National Council
on Economic Education

THE EconomicsAmerica® AND EconomicsInternational® PROGRAMS

voluntary

NATIONAL CONTENT STANDARDS IN ECONOMICS

Developed by

National Council on Economic Education

in partnership with

National Association of Economic Educators

Foundation for Teaching Economics

PROJECT DIRECTOR

Bonnie Meszaros
Center for Economic Education and Entrepreneurship
University of Delaware

WRITING COMMITTEE

John Siegfried, Chair
Vanderbilt University

James Charkins
Center for Economic Education
University of California, San Bernardino

Nancy Hanlon
Willow Elementary School
Homewood, Illinois

Robert Highsmith
Pace University

Donna McCreadie
Temple City High School
Temple City, California

Bonnie Meszaros
Center for Economic Education and Entrepreneurship
University of Delaware

Robert Smith
Texas Council on Economic Education

Mary Suiter
Center for Entrepreneurship and Economic Education
University of Missouri, St. Louis

Gary Walton
Foundation for Teaching Economics

Michael Watts
Center for Economic Education
Purdue University

Donald Wentworth
Center for Economic Education
Pacific Lutheran University

STEERING COMMITTEE

James Charkins
Center for Economic Education
University of California, San Bernardino

W. Lee Hansen
University of Wisconsin

Robert Reinke
South Dakota Council on Economic Education

Michael Salemi
University of North Carolina, Chapel Hill

John Siegfried
Vanderbilt University

Gary Walton
Foundation for Teaching Economics

REVIEW COMMITTEE

Michael Salemi, Chair
University of North Carolina, Chapel Hill

William Baumol
New York University and
Professor Emeritus, Princeton University

William Darity
University of North Carolina, Chapel Hill

Claudia Goldin
Harvard University

John Taylor
Stanford University

TEACHER USER COMMITTEE

Laurie Engstrom
Charter School, Wilmington, Delaware

Sally Finch
Westminster Schools, Atlanta, Georgia

Nancy Hanlon
Willow Elementary School,
Homewood, Illinois

Donna McCreadie
Temple City High School,
Temple City, California

Donna Wright
Baker Elementary School,
Little Rock, Arkansas

Larry Yarrell
Lawrence North High School,
Indianapolis, Indiana

IMPLEMENTATION COMMITTEE

Gail Funk Colbert
Minnesota Council on Economic Education

Robert Reinke
South Dakota Council on Economic Education

DeVon Yoho
Center for Economic Education
Ball State University

ACKNOWLEDGMENTS

Many individuals reviewed the drafts of the *Voluntary National Content Standards in Economics*. In addition, many members of professional organizations and participants at national and regional meetings reviewed the economic standards. These individuals and organizations are listed below. We are grateful for their help.

William Becker, Indiana University

Stephen Buckles, Vanderbilt University

Michael MacDowell, Calvin K. Kazanjian Economics Foundation, Inc.

Claire Melican, National Council on Economic Education

John Morton, Arizona Council on Economic Education Scottsdale, Arizona

National Association of Business Economists

National Association of Economic Educators

National Council on Economic Education's Network of Affiliated Councils and Centers

National Council on Economic Education's Board of Founders

National Council for the Social Studies

E. Angus Powell Invisible Hand Conference Participants

Readers of the Economic Advanced Placement Exams, 1996

State Social Studies Directors

University of Delaware's Master of Arts in Economics for Educators, Class of 1997

Richard Western, University of Wisconsin–Milwaukee

FUNDING

Funding for this project came from the Calvin K. Kazanjian Economics Foundation, Inc., the AT&T Foundation, and the Foundation for Teaching Economics. Their generous and timely support is most gratefully acknowledged.

CONTENTS

CONTENTS

FOREWORD

The purpose of the *Voluntary National Content Standards in Economics* is to help raise the quality of economic education in America's schools.

Standards in economics are for students entering a complex global economy, so that they may fully and effectively participate in it. The standards are the result of more than a decade of general concern on the part of educators and other citizens regarding educational reform in the United States. The standards are benchmarks, guides, concepts that foster and fortify incremental learning experiences. Standards are not hurdles to be overcome. They are signposts to point the way to economic literacy, not to circumscribe it.

The *Voluntary National Content Standards in Economics* provide a tool for educators, specifying what students, kindergarten through grade 12, should learn about basic economics and the economy as they go through school, so that they will be better informed workers, consumers and producers, savers and investors, and most important, citizens.

The fact that economics is one of nine subject areas in the *Goals 2000: Educate America Act* of 1994 demonstrates its importance as a core subject in American schools. The standards are designed purposefully to advance economic literacy, which is critically important for the future of our students— who are our future.

There are four attributes of these standards in economics for readers and users to keep in mind:

First, the standards are written for teachers; they have instructional value.

Second, the standards are written for teachers to use in practice; they outline benchmarks, guides to application, and teaching suggestions and strategies, in the belief that all students can learn and that learning principles of economics can be enjoyable, not dismal.

Third, the standards are written for teachers to use to help students learn crucial reasoning and decision-making skills that will serve them well all of their lives, in all of the many roles that they may play as responsible and effective participants in the American economic system.

Fourth, the standards are well-written and clear, benefiting from the insights and critiques of numerous educators and economists across the nation; they are a high-quality product—that is, made to serve their purpose, made to last, and made with distinction.

The standards in economics are commended to all who see measures of attainable knowledge as important to the growth of individuals and the health of society and who believe with Jefferson that an educated and literate—and, we would now add, economically literate—citizenry is essential for democracy to survive and to thrive.

Robert F. Duvall, President & CEO
National Council on Economic Education

PREFACE

After economics was included in the Goals 2000 Educate America Act in 1994, the National Council on Economic Education (NCEE) assembled a coalition of organizations to write voluntary content standards to guide economics instruction in American schools. The coalition includes representatives from the NCEE and its network of affiliated councils and centers, the National Association of Economic Educators, the Foundation for Teaching Economics, and the American Economic Association's Committee on Economic Education. Financial support for the effort was provided by the Calvin K. Kazanjian Economics Foundation, Inc., the AT&T Foundation, and the Foundation for Teaching Economics. In addition to financial support, many individuals generously contributed their time to produce these standards.

WRITING COMMITTEE

The coalition established a Writing Committee that prepared these national voluntary economics content standards. The Writing Committee consisted of John Siegfried (Vanderbilt University, chair), Bonnie Meszaros, University of Delaware, project director), James Charkins (California State University-San Bernardino), Nancy Hanlon (Willow School, Homewood, Illinois), Robert Highsmith (Pace University), Donna McCreadie (Temple City High School, Temple City, California), Robert Smith (Texas Council on Economic Education), Mary Suiter (University of Missouri-St. Louis), Gary Walton (University of California-Davis and the Foundation for Teaching Economics), Michael Watts (Purdue University), and Donald Wentworth (Pacific Lutheran University).

The entire Writing Committee met three times for two days each between October 1995 and July 1996. There were several additional meetings of subcommittees. The standards went through about 10 drafts. The drafts were reviewed by the Writing Committee, people representing a variety of organizations, individual professional economists, and teachers. A formal Review Committee of professional economists read an intermediate draft and offered comments and advice that greatly improved the economic content of the standards. Members of this Review Committee were Michael Salemi (University of

North Carolina, chair), William Baumol (Princeton University and New York University), William Darity (University of North Carolina), Claudia Goldin (Harvard University), and John Taylor (Stanford University).

This publication reports the fruits of this substantial effort. There are 20 economics content standards. Each standard is an essential principle of economics that an economically literate student should know and a statement of what the student should be able to do with that knowledge upon graduating from high school. This knowledge includes the most important and enduring ideas, concepts, and issues in economics.

BENCHMARKS

Each standard is accompanied by a rationale for its inclusion. The rationale explains to educators, parents, and citizens why it is essential for students to understand that standard, and how the students' lives and the lives of other citizens improve with that understanding. In addition, each standard also includes a set of benchmarks, divided into grades 4, 8, and 12 achievement levels. The benchmarks identify building blocks underlying the principles embedded in the standard. They contain assumptions, intermediate conclusions, and elaborations for each standard. To a large extent, the benchmarks develop the economic reasoning behind the standard. In this way, the standards and benchmarks add up to more than a simple list of "things to know." As students observe the reasoning process used by economists and practice it themselves, they will acquire analytical skills they can apply to emerging economic issues unforeseen at the time these standards were written.

INSTRUCTIONAL RESOURCES

The economics content standards are coordinated with instructional resources. Each benchmark is accompanied with suggested exercises a teacher might use to help students understand the benchmark. In addition, the NCEE has a long history of producing economic education instructional materials for grades K-12. When these are integrated with the content standards, teachers have access to a package that both articulates the goals of economics instruction and provides the means to achieve the goals.

The standards are primarily conceptual. They do not include important basic facts about the American and world economies. The introduction to the standards indicates, however, that students also should know some pertinent facts about the American economy, including its size and the current rates of unemployment, inflation, and interest. Many of the exercises suggested in the benchmarks lead students to acquire such information. The relevant facts students should know about the economy change constantly, however. Conceptual standards, on the other hand, highlight the unique contribution of economics and are enduring principles. They also facilitate an emphasis on economic reasoning, encouraging students to develop the capacity to deduce conclusions from whatever facts are pertinent to the myriad of problems they will confront in their lives.

THE LANGUAGE OF ECONOMICS

The standards were written so that parents, teachers, students, and the general public can understand what they mean and what the standards require students to do. Although the nomenclature of economics is avoided in the standards, much of the language of economics, as well as many of the principles of economics, are contained in the benchmarks. Terms such as opportunity cost, marginal cost, transactions costs, comparative advantage, equilibrium, externalities, public goods, and potential gross domestic product appear only in benchmarks. Some other important language of economics, for example, economies of scale and the multiplier, do not appear at all, although those concepts are included in more accessible language.

Still other common economic concepts that are invariably included in introductory college economics courses are not in the standards at all. These include, for example, income effects, elasticity, absolute advantage, and diminishing marginal returns.

Before a concept was included in the standards or benchmarks, the Writing Committee asked why it was *essential* for a high school graduate to understand it. Understanding each standard should be necessary for citizenship, employment, and/or life-long learning of economics, and help a typical high school graduate grapple with the ordinary business of life. When the Committee could not explain satisfactorily why the concept was essential, or if there was doubt, especially when the concept is difficult to convey, the concept was excluded.

BEST SCHOLARSHIP IN THE DISCIPLINE

The standards attempt to reflect consensus in the discipline. This goal was accomplished by using the majority paradigm, circulating the standards widely, and considering comments and advice from readers of various drafts. The final standards reflect the view of a large majority of economists today in favor of a "neoclassical model" of economic behavior. The Committee's use of this paradigm does not connote a repudiation of alternatives. Rather, it reflects the assignment to produce a single, coherent set of standards to guide the teaching of economics in America's schools. Including strongly held minority views of economic processes risks confusing and frustrating teachers and students who are then left with the responsibility of sorting the qualifications and alternatives without a sufficient foundation to do so.

The standards are supposed to be correct, and to reflect the best scholarship in the discipline. This criterion turned out to be challenging. In areas of controversy, for example, macroeconomics, the Committee struggled to identify a consensus paradigm, and probably some economists will conclude that it failed. More difficult, however, was balancing the trade-off between accuracy and parsimony. Almost all economics principles are conditioned on assumptions. To report all of those assumptions each time would detract from the effectiveness of the standards, as readers would be left with the responsibility of distinguishing the principle from the assumptions. So, in numerous cases, without specifying all of the required assumptions, standards and benchmarks imply as always true some principles that are widely agreed to be true most, but not necessarily all, of the time.

FUNDAMENTAL ECONOMIC IDEAS AND CONCEPTS

The standards focus on the more fundamental economic ideas and concepts that are widely shared by professional economists. Some very important aspects of economics are either quite complex or so controversial that there seems to be no existing consensus. In spite of their importance, such complex or controversial aspects of economics receive less attention in the standards for pedagogical reasons. In addition, those aspects of economics that are more easily separated into independent components account for more of the standards. For these reasons, there are relatively more standards about microeconomics than macroeconomics. The individual macroeconomics standards, however, are quite significant for the many citizenship, employment, and financial decisions a typical high school graduate will confront during his or her lifetime.

In addition to the members of the Writing Committee and the Review Committee already identified, we owe considerable appreciation for contributed time and effort to all those people whose generous comments and suggestions helped to shape this document. They are too numerous to list. We note especially the assistance of Stephen Buckles, W. Lee Hansen, and William Walstad, who read numerous drafts of the standards and contributed throughout the process.

These national voluntary content standards for pre-college economics education should make it easier to incorporate the powerful fundamental principles of economics into elementary and secondary school curricula. They are offered as a resource for states and local school districts, for individual schools, and for teachers, who are the people ultimately responsible for specifying and integrating the curriculum into their schools.

Bonnie T. Meszaros
John J. Siegfried

INTRODUCTION: VOLUNTARY NATIONAL CONTENT STANDARDS IN ECONOMICS

The inclusion of economics as a core subject in the *Goals 2000: Educate America Act* recognizes the value of economic understanding in helping people comprehend the modern world, make decisions that shape the future, and strengthen major institutions. The principles of economics bear directly on the ordinary business of life, affecting people in their roles as consumers and producers. Economics also plays an important role in local, state, national, and international public policy. Economic issues frequently influence voters in national, state, and local elections. A better understanding of economics enables people to understand the forces that affect them every day and helps them identify and evaluate the consequences of private decisions and public policies. Many institutions of a democratic market economy function more effectively when its citizens are articulate and well informed about economics.

Learning how to reason about economic issues is important also because the analytic approach of economics differs in key respects from approaches appropriate for other related subjects such as history and civics. Yet valid economic analysis helps us to master such subjects as well, providing effective ways to examine many of the "why" questions in history, politics, business, and international relations.

Skills, as well as content, play an important part in economic reasoning. The key skills students must develop in economics include an ability to (a) identify economic problems, alternatives, benefits, and costs; (b) analyze the incentives at work in an economic situation; (c) examine the consequences of changes in economic conditions and public policies; (d) collect and organize economic evidence; and (e) compare benefits with costs.

Students should have gained several kinds of economic knowledge by the time they have finished the twelfth grade. First, they should understand basic economic concepts and be able to reason logically about key economic issues that affect their lives as workers, consumers, and citizens, so they can avoid errors that are common among persons who do not understand economics. Second, they should know some pertinent facts about the American economy, including its size and the current rates of unemployment, inflation, and interest. Third, they should understand that there are differing views on some economic issues. This is especially true for topics such as the appropriate size of government in a market economy, how and when the federal government should try to fight unemployment and inflation, and how and when the federal government should try to promote economic growth. Nevertheless, on many issues and in basic methods of analysis, there is widespread agreement among economists.

The essential principles of economics are identified in the 20 content standards that follow. Each standard is followed by a rationale for its inclusion. Then benchmarks for the teaching of each of the content standards are provided, indicating recommended levels of attainment for students in grades 4, 8, and 12. Finally, samples of what students can do to enhance or demonstrate their understanding of the benchmarks are provided.

Content Standard 1

Students will understand that:

Productive resources are limited. Therefore, people cannot have all the goods and services they want; as a result, they must choose some things and give up others.

Students will be able to use this knowledge to:

Identify what they gain and what they give up when they make choices.

Students face many choices every day. Is watching TV the best use of their time? Is working at a fast-food restaurant better than the best alternative job or some other use of their time? Identifying and systematically comparing alternatives enables people to make informed decisions and to avoid unforeseen consequences of choices they or others make.

Some students believe they can have all the goods and services they want from their families or from the government because goods provided by families or governments are free. But this view is mistaken. Resources have alternative uses, even if parents or governments own them. For example, if a city uses land to build a football stadium, the best alternative use of that land must be given up. If additional funds are budgeted for police patrols, less money is available to hire more teachers. Explicitly comparing the value of alternative opportunities that are sacrificed in any choice enables citizens and their political representatives to weigh the alternatives in order to make better economic decisions. This analysis also makes people aware of the consequences of their actions for themselves and others, and leads to a heightened sense of responsibility and accountability.

BENCHMARKS

At the completion of **Grade 4**, *students will know that:*

1. People make choices because they cannot have everything they want.
2. Economic wants are desires that can be satisfied by consuming a good, service, or leisure activity.
3. Goods are objects that can satisfy people's wants.
4. Services are actions that can satisfy people's wants.
5. People's choices about what goods and services to buy and consume determine how resources will be used.
6. Whenever a choice is made, something is given up.
7. The opportunity cost of a choice is the value of the best alternative given up.
8. People whose wants are satisfied by using goods and services are called consumers.
9. Productive resources are the natural resources, human resources, and capital goods available to make goods and services.
10. Natural resources, such as land, are "gifts of nature"; they are present without human intervention.
11. Human resources are the quantity and quality of human effort directed toward producing goods and services.
12. Capital goods are goods produced and used to make other goods and services.

13. Human capital refers to the quality of labor resources, which can be improved through investments in education, training, and health.

14. Entrepreneurs are people who organize other productive resources to make goods and services.

15. People who make goods and provide services are called producers.

*At the completion of **Grade 4**, students will use this knowledge to:*

1. Identify some choices they have made and explain why they had to make a choice.

2. Match a list of wants with the correct example of a good, service, or leisure activity that satisfies each want.

3. Create a collage representing goods that they or their families consume.

4. Create a collage representing services that they or their families consume.

5. Explain why a choice must be made, given some land and a list of alternative uses for the land.

6. Choose a toy from a list of four toys and state what was given up.

7. Describe a situation that requires a choice, make a decision, and identify the opportunity cost.

8. Examine pictorial examples of people using goods and services and identify the goods and services being consumed.

9. Identify examples of natural resources, human resources, and capital goods used in the production of a given product.

10. Use a resource map of their state to locate examples of natural resources.

11. Draw pictures representing themselves as workers. Also, identify examples of human resources used in the production of education at their school.

12. Draw a picture representing a capital good used at school. Also, identify examples of capital goods used to produce goods or services in their community.

13. Give examples of how to improve their human capital. Explain how an athlete invests in his or her human capital.

14. Select an entrepreneur and identify the productive resources the entrepreneur uses to produce a good or service.

15. Identify producers of five different types of goods and five different types of services.

*At the completion of **Grade 8**, students will know the Grade 4 benchmarks for this standard and also that:*

1. Scarcity is the condition of not being able to have all of the goods and services one wants. It exists because human wants for goods and services exceed the quantity of goods and services that can be produced using all available resources.

2. Like individuals, governments and societies experience scarcity because human wants exceed what can be made from all available resources.

3. Choices involve trading off the expected value of one opportunity against the expected value of its best alternative.

4. The choices people make have both present and future consequences.

5. The evaluation of choices and opportunity costs is subjective; such evaluations differ across individuals and societies.

*At the completion of **Grade 8**, students will use this knowledge to:*

1. Work in groups each representing a scout troop that has volunteered to assist a local nursing home on Saturday morning. The nursing home has a list of 30 possible projects, all of which it would like completed. Explain why all 30 projects cannot be completed on a Saturday morning.

2. Role play a city council meeting called to allocate a budget of $100,000. The council would like to buy four new police cars at $25,000 each, repair two senior-citizen centers at $50,000 each, and build two new tennis courts at $50,000 each. Explain why a choice must be made, decide how the city council should spend its money, describe the trade-offs made, and identify the opportunity cost of the decision.

3. Determine criteria for selecting a stereo and identify the trade-offs made when selecting one stereo over another.

4. Analyze the consequences of choosing not to study for a final exam and tell when those consequences occur.

5. Individually develop a solution to a problem that affects everybody in the class and identify the opportunity cost. Compare the solutions and explain why solutions and opportunity costs differ among students.

*At the completion of **Grade 12**, students will know the Grade 4 and Grade 8 benchmarks for this standard and also that:*

1. Choices made by individuals, firms, or government officials often have long-run unintended consequences that can partially or entirely offset the initial effects of their decisions.

*At the completion of **Grade 12**, students will use this knowledge to:*

1. Explain how a high school senior's decision to work 20 hours per week during the school year could reduce her lifetime income. Also, explain how an increase in the legal minimum wage aimed at improving the financial condition of some low-income families could reduce the income of some minimum wage earners.

Content Standard 2

Students will understand that:

Effective decision making requires comparing the additional costs of alternatives with the additional benefits. Most choices involve doing a little more or a little less of something; few choices are all-or-nothing decisions.

Students will be able to use this knowledge to:

Make effective decisions as consumers, producers, savers, investors, and citizens.

To make decisions that provide the greatest possible return from the resources available, people and organizations must weigh the benefits and costs of using their resources to do a little more of some things and a little less of others. For example, to use their time effectively, students must weigh the additional benefits and costs of spending another hour studying economics rather than listening to music or talking with friends. School officials must decide whether to use some school funds to buy more books for the library, more helmets for the football team, or more equipment for teachers to use in their classrooms. Company managers and directors must choose which products to make and whether to increase or decrease the amount they produce. The President, Congress, and other government officials must decide which public spending programs to increase and which ones to decrease.

Focusing on changes in benefits and comparing them to changes in costs is a way of thinking that distinguishes economics from most social sciences. In applying this approach, students should realize that it is impossible to alter how resources were used in the past. Instead, past decisions only establish the starting points for current decisions about whether to increase, decrease, or leave unchanged resource levels devoted to different activities.

BENCHMARKS

*At the completion of **Grade 4**, students will know that:*
1. Few choices are all-or-nothing decisions; they usually involve getting a little more of one thing by giving up a little of something else.
2. A cost is what you give up when you decide to do something.
3. A benefit is something that satisfies your wants.

*At the completion of **Grade 4**, students will use this knowledge to:*
1. Analyze how to divide their time on a Saturday afternoon when the possibilities are raking leaves to earn money, going roller skating with friends, and shopping at the mall with their aunt. Students will identify the possible uses of their time and explain how devoting more time to one activity leaves less time for another.
2. List the costs of buying and caring for a pet.
3. List the benefits of buying and caring for a pet.

*At the completion of **Grade 8**, students will know the Grade 4 benchmarks for this standard and also that:*
1. To determine the best level of consumption of a product, people must compare the additional benefits with the additional costs of consuming a little more or a little less.

*At the completion of **Grade 8**, students will use this knowledge to:*
1. Solve the following problem: Your grandmother gave you $30 for your birthday and you are trying to decide how to spend it. You are considering buying compact discs ($12 each), going to the movies ($5 per ticket), or taking some friends out for pizza ($7.50 per person). You do not have to spend all your money on one thing. You can use some money for one thing and some for another. How would you spend your money to get the greatest satisfaction?

*At the completion of **Grade 12**, students will know the Grade 4 and 8 benchmarks for this standard and also that:*
1. Marginal benefit is the change in total benefit resulting from an action. Marginal cost is the change in total cost resulting from an action.
2. As long as the marginal benefit of an activity exceeds the marginal cost, people are better off doing more of it; when the marginal cost exceeds the marginal benefit, they are better off doing less of it.

3. To produce the profit-maximizing level of output and hire the optimal number of workers and other resources, producers must compare the marginal benefits and marginal costs of producing a little more with the marginal benefits and marginal costs of producing a little less.

4. To determine the optimal level of a public policy program, voters and government officials must compare the marginal benefits and marginal costs of providing a little more or a little less of the program's services.

*At the completion of **Grade 12**, students will use this knowledge to:*

1. Explain why beyond some point they are unwilling to buy and consume an additional slice of pizza.

2. Apply the concepts of marginal benefit and marginal cost to an environmental policy to find the optimal amount of pollution for two firms that have substantially different costs of reducing pollution.

3. Decide how many workers to hire for a profit-maximizing car wash by comparing the cost of hiring each additional worker to the additional revenues derived from hiring each additional worker.

4. Use the concepts of marginal cost and marginal benefit to evaluate proposals for a pollution-control ordinance aimed at maximizing economic efficiency; then select the best proposal and explain why it seems best.

Content Standard 3

Students will understand that:

Different methods can be used to allocate goods and services. People, acting individually or collectively through government, must choose which methods to use to allocate different kinds of goods and services.

Students will be able to use this knowledge to:

Evaluate different methods of allocating goods and services by comparing the benefits and costs of each method.

Individuals and organizations routinely use different decision-making systems to determine what should be produced, how it should be produced, and who will consume it. Most high school students already understand the major advantages and disadvantages of selling concert tickets using a first-come-first-served system, rather than a lottery, to select from among those who applied for tickets. Unfortunately, many students have experienced the use of force to allocate resources on the school playground. Students also know that families typically use authoritarian systems to decide how resources are used—that is, Mom and/or Dad decide.

The American economy uses a market system to make many allocation decisions, and it is important for students to understand why the market system is used so extensively. Students also should be able to compare the characteristics of a market system with alternatives used more extensively in some other countries. With this understanding, students can assess the benefits and costs of alternative allocation systems when discussing difficult questions such as how incomes should be divided among people or who should receive a kidney transplant and who should not.

BENCHMARKS

At the completion of **Grade 4***, students will know that:*

1. No method of distributing goods and services can satisfy all wants.

2. There are different ways to distribute goods and services (by prices, command, majority rule, contests, force, first-come-first-served, sharing equally, lottery, personal characteristics, and others), and there are advantages and disadvantages to each.

At the completion of **Grade 4***, students will use this knowledge to:*

1. Generate different methods for allocating student time on classroom computers, tell who gains and who loses with each distribution method, and conclude that no distribution method satisfies all wants.

2. Compare the advantages and disadvantages of different methods of allocating various goods and services, such as cookies, houses, student time on playground equipment at recess, elective class offices, military service in times of war or peace, and athletic championships.

At the completion of **Grade 8***, students will know the Grade 4 benchmarks for this standard and also that:*

1. Scarcity requires the use of some distribution method, whether the method is selected explicitly or not.

2. There are essential differences between a market economy, in which allocations result from individuals making decisions as buyers and sellers, and a command economy, in which resources are allocated according to central authority.

3. People in all economies must answer three basic questions: What goods and services will be produced? How will these goods and services be produced? Who will consume them?

4. National economies vary in the extent to which they rely on government directives (central planning) and signals from private markets to allocate scarce goods, services, and productive resources.

5. As consumers, people use resources in different ways to satisfy different wants. Productive resources can be used in different ways to produce different goods and services.

At the completion of **Grade 8***, students will use this knowledge to:*

1. Describe the distribution methods used to allocate a variety of goods and services, such as parking spaces, prison paroles, access to a new drug treatment for cancer, seats on a bus, milk, and tickets to a popular art exhibit. Then explain why a distribution method is necessary.

2. Compare the methods used to allocate work responsibilities in homes with those used to allocate work responsibilities in businesses. Also, compare the advantages and disadvantages of economic systems used in different countries and at different times, using as criteria broad social goals such as freedom, efficiency, fairness, and growth.

3. Answer the three economic questions while producing a simple classroom product, such as yarn bracelets, greeting cards, or decorations for a school dance.

4. Compare the relative size and responsibilities of government in several countries.

5. List the resources used to produce some item and identify other items that could have been made from these resources.

*At the completion of **Grade 12**, students will know the Grade 4 and 8 benchmarks for this standard and also that:*

1. Comparing the benefits and costs of different allocation methods in order to choose the method that is most appropriate for some specific problem can result in more effective allocations and a more effective overall allocation system.

*At the completion of **Grade 12**, students will use this knowledge to:*

1. Examine economic systems used in different countries, select the one that provides the most effective method for allocating resources, and explain why this method is effective. Also, assess the effectiveness of various systems for allocating organ transplants, hunting and fishing licenses, elective offices, time with a parent, and access to hospital maternity facilities.

Content Standard 4

Students will understand that:

People respond predictably to positive and negative incentives.

Students will be able to use this knowledge to:

Identify incentives that affect people's behavior and explain how incentives affect their own behavior.

Economic incentives are the additional rewards or penalties people receive from engaging in more or less of a particular activity. Understanding rewards and penalties helps people to make the choices they need to make in order to achieve their goals. Prices, wages, profits, subsidies, and taxes are common economic incentives. Subsidizing an activity usually leads to more of it being provided; taxing or penalizing an activity usually leads to less of it being provided.

People frequently have good reasons to influence the behavior of others. For example, businesses try to encourage people to buy more of their products, workers try to persuade employers to hire them and to pay them higher wages, and governments try to induce the production and consumption of some products and discourage the production and consumption of others. To understand or predict the behavior of people or organizations, students must understand the economic incentives these people or organizations face.

BENCHMARKS

*At the completion of **Grade 4**, students will know that:*

1. Rewards are positive incentives that make people better off.
2. Penalties are negative incentives that make people worse off.
3. Both positive and negative incentives affect people's choices and behavior.
4. People's views of rewards and penalties differ because people have different values. Therefore, an incentive can influence different individuals in different ways.

*At the completion of **Grade 4**, students will use this knowledge to:*

1. List examples of rewards that are incentives for positive classroom behavior.

2. List examples of penalties or negative incentives that discourage inappropriate behavior at home.

3. Identify examples of incentives and categorize them as positive or negative incentives.

4. Identify the incentives that would encourage them to read a book, to return their library books on time, to repay money they borrow from the school cafeteria for lunch, and to complete their homework assignments on time; explain why various students respond differently to incentives to do these things. Also, explain why some students will do extra-credit work and some will not.

*At the completion of **Grade 8**, students will know the Grade 4 benchmarks for this standard and also that:*

1. Responses to incentives are predictable because people usually pursue their self-interest.

2. Changes in incentives cause people to change their behavior in predictable ways.

3. Incentives can be monetary or non-monetary.

*At the completion of **Grade 8**, students will use this knowledge to:*

1. Explain why they would be willing to shovel snow when temperatures are below freezing, mow lawns when their friends are going to a movie, or babysit on a weekend evening instead of going with friends to a dance.

2. Predict how students' study habits will change if the grading system changes from letter grades to pass/fail to no grades.

3. Identify the monetary and non-monetary incentives related to taking a driver's education class.

*At the completion of **Grade 12**, students will know the Grade 4 and 8 benchmarks for this standard and also that:*

1. Acting as consumers, producers, workers, savers, investors, and citizens, people respond to incentives in order to allocate their scarce resources in ways that provide the highest possible returns to them.

2. Small and large firms, labor unions, and educational and other not-for-profit organizations have different goals and face different rules and constraints. These goals, rules, and constraints influence the benefits and costs of those who work with or for those organizations and, therefore, their behavior.

*At the completion of **Grade 12**, students will use this knowledge to:*

1. Analyze the impact (on consumers, producers, workers, savers, and investors) of an increase in the minimum wage, a new tax policy, or a change in interest rates.

2. Compare and contrast the incentives an individual might face in serving as an elected official, the owner of a small business, the president of a large company, and the director of a local United Way office.

Content Standard 5

Students will understand that:

Voluntary exchange occurs only when all participating parties expect to gain. This is true for trade among individuals or organizations within a nation, and among individuals or organizations in different nations.

Students will be able to use this knowledge to:

Negotiate exchanges and identify the gains to themselves and others. Compare the benefits and costs of policies that alter trade barriers between nations, such as tariffs and quotas.

As a result of their competitive experiences in sports and games, students usually have learned to expect that, in most contests, when one person or team wins, another person or team must lose. Voluntary exchanges, on the other hand, are cooperative activities in which both sides expect to gain, and both usually do. Because all the parties to a voluntary exchange expect to gain from trade, institutions that make trading easier usually improve social welfare.

Understanding the win-win nature of voluntary exchange helps students learn that people and organizations trade with one another only when each party offers something that the other party values more than whatever he or she has to trade. For example, an employer will hire a student at a wage rate of $6 per hour only if the employer expects to receive labor services from the student that are worth at least that much. And the student will voluntarily work for $6 per hour only if the student values the $6 more than the best alternative use of his or her time. The principle that voluntary trade can improve each participant's situation applies to all voluntary exchanges, including trade between people or organizations in different parts of the same country or among people or organizations in different countries.

BENCHMARKS

*At the completion of **Grade 4**, students will know that:*

1. Exchange is trading goods and services with people for other goods and services or for money.
2. The oldest form of exchange is barter—the direct trading of goods and services between people.
3. People voluntarily exchange goods and services because they expect to be better off after the exchange.

*At the completion of **Grade 4**, students will use this knowledge to:*

1. Identify exchanges they have made and tell whether they were monetary or barter exchanges.
2. Identify current and historical examples of barter exchanges.
3. Describe a trade they have made, such as one with baseball cards, stickers, or lunch desserts, and explain why they agreed to trade.

At the completion of **Grade 8**, *students will know the Grade 4 benchmarks for this standard and also that:*

1. When people buy something, they value it more than whatever it costs them; when people sell something, they value it less than the payment they receive.

2. Free trade increases worldwide material standards of living.

3. Despite the mutual benefits from trade among people in different countries, many nations employ trade barriers to restrict free trade for national defense reasons or because some companies and workers are hurt by free trade.

4. Imports are foreign goods and services purchased from sellers in other nations.

5. Exports are domestic goods and services sold to buyers in other nations.

6. Voluntary exchange among people or organizations in different countries gives people a broader range of choices in buying goods and services.

At the completion of **Grade 8**, *students will use this knowledge to:*

1. Describe recent monetary transactions they have made; as buyers or sellers, explain why they were willing to trade.

2. Identify the benefits when a trade barrier such as sugar or automobile import quotas is eliminated.

3. Look at historical examples of periods when the United States has imposed trade barriers and explain why U. S. citizens would impose trade barriers, given the mutual benefits of free trade.

4. Examine labels of products in their homes to compile a list of imported products and identify the countries from which they are imported.

5. Determine what major products are produced in their community for export and the countries to which they are exported.

6. Describe how their daily lives would be different if people in the United States did not trade with people in other countries.

At the completion of **Grade 12**, *students will know the Grade 4 and 8 benchmarks for this standard and also that:*

1. A nation pays for its imports with its exports.

2. When imports are restricted by public policies, consumers pay higher prices and job opportunities and profits in exporting firms decrease.

At the completion of **Grade 12**, *students will use this knowledge to:*

1. Participate in a trading simulation where students represent different countries with specific goods to sell and specific goods they wish to buy; conclude that a nation pays for its imports with its exports, or by borrowing.

2. Analyze the political and economic implications of a proposed ban on imported television sets.

Content Standard 6

Students will understand that:

When individuals, regions, and nations specialize in what they can produce at the lowest cost and then trade with others, both production and consumption increase.

Students will be able to use this knowledge to:

Explain how they can benefit themselves and others by developing special skills and strengths.

Everyone specializes to some degree, and everyone depends on others to produce many of the things he or she consumes. As future producers and workers, students should understand that they will earn more by specializing in doing the things they can do well and that entail the least sacrifice in forgone opportunities. They also should understand that specialization can lead to increased production, even when everyone has similar skills and resources, because concentrating production of some goods or services in one location can sometimes reduce production costs.

This understanding will help students appreciate why an economy in which people specialize and trade voluntarily with one another results in higher overall levels of production and consumption, for individuals, regions, and nations.

BENCHMARKS

*At the completion of **Grade 4**, students will know that:*

1. Economic specialization occurs when people concentrate their production on fewer kinds of goods and services than they consume.
2. Division of labor occurs when the production of a good is broken down into numerous separate tasks, with different workers performing each task.
3. Specialization and division of labor usually increase the productivity of workers.
4. Greater specialization leads to increased interdependence among producers and consumers.

*At the completion of **Grade 4**, students will use this knowledge to:*

1. Name several adults in the school or community who specialize in the production of a good or service (e.g., baker, law enforcement officer, teacher, etc.), and identify other goods and services that these individuals consume but do not produce for themselves.
2. Participate in a simulated assembly line and identify the separate operations and the different tasks involved.
3. Work individually to produce a product and then work as a member of a small group to produce the same product. Explain why more goods usually are produced when each member of the group performs a particular task in making the good.
4. Compare the extent of specialization and interdependence of a shipwrecked sailor living on an isolated Pacific island with a family that owns a cattle ranch in New Mexico.

*At the completion of **Grade 8**, students will know the Grade 4 benchmarks for this standard and also that:*

1. Labor productivity is output per worker.

2. Like trade among individuals within one country, international trade promotes specialization and division of labor and increases output and consumption.

3. As a result of growing international economic interdependence, economic conditions and policies in one nation increasingly affect economic conditions and policies in other nations.

>*At the completion of **Grade 8**, students will use this knowledge to:*
>
>1. Produce a product using a simulated assembly line process and compute output per worker.
>
>2. Explain why Canada produces relatively more ice hockey players and the United States produces relatively more baseball players.
>
>3. Explain how a tariff on imported cacao beans affects the production of chocolate candy in the United States and how it affects people in cacao-growing countries. Also, analyze data on the kinds and value of goods that Japan, Canada, Mexico, and Germany export to the United States and predict the likely effect of a recession in the United States on the economies of these countries.

*At the completion of **Grade 12**, students will know the Grade 4 and 8 benchmarks for this standard and also that:*

1. Two factors that prompt international trade are international differences in the availability of productive resources and differences in relative prices.

2. Transaction costs are costs (other than price) that are associated with the purchase of a good or service. When transaction costs decrease, trade increases.

3. Individuals and nations have a comparative advantage in the production of goods or services if they can produce a product at a lower opportunity cost than other individuals or nations.

4. Comparative advantages change over time because of changes in factor endowments, resource prices, and events that occur in other nations.

>*At the completion of **Grade 12**, students will use this knowledge to:*
>
>1. Name three things, such as bananas, coffee, and Eucalyptus oil, that could be produced in the continental United States, although production would be very costly, and explain in terms of opportunity costs why the United States is probably better off importing such goods.
>
>2. Identify transaction costs associated with the purchase of a good or service. Also, explain why each of the following encourages exchange: (1) more efficient trucks that can carry larger loads for the same fuel costs; (2) automated teller machines; (3) credit cards; and (4) classified advertising.
>
>3. Apply the concepts of opportunity cost and comparative advantage to the following problem: The Netherlands can produce in one day either four drill presses or eight embroidered tablecloths. Using the same amount of resources, Portugal can produce either two drill presses or seven embroidered tablecloths. Which country should specialize in drill presses and import tablecloths, and why? Which country should specialize in tablecloths and import drill presses, and why?
>
>4. Explain why the United States no longer has a comparative advantage in the production of shoes.

Content Standard 7

Students will understand that:

Markets exist when buyers and sellers interact. This interaction determines market prices and thereby allocates scarce goods and services.

Students will be able to use this knowledge to:

Identify markets in which they have participated as a buyer and a seller and describe how the interaction of all buyers and sellers influences prices. Also, predict how prices change when there is either a shortage or surplus of the product available.

In market economies there is no central planning agency that decides how many different kinds of sandwiches are provided for lunch every day at restaurants and stores, how many loaves of bread are baked, how many toys are produced before the holidays, or what the prices will be for the sandwiches, bread, and toys. Students should understand that, instead, most prices in market economies are established by interaction between buyers and sellers.

Understanding how market prices and output levels are determined helps people anticipate market opportunities and make better choices as consumers and producers. It will also help them realize that market allocations are impersonal.

BENCHMARKS

*At the completion of **Grade 4**, students will know that:*

1. A price is what people pay when they buy a good or service, and what they receive when they sell a good or service.
2. A market exists whenever buyers and sellers exchange goods and services.
3. Most people both produce and consume. As producers they make goods and services; as consumers they use goods and services.

*At the completion of **Grade 4**, students will use this knowledge to:*

1. Identify prices they have paid for a hamburger, french fries, and a soda, and prices they have received for selling lemonade, feeding a neighbor's pet while its owner is on vacation, or doing certain household chores.
2. Give examples of markets in which buyers and sellers meet face-to-face, and other markets in which buyers and sellers never meet.
3. Identify people who are acting as consumers, and provide examples of situations in which the students were consumers of goods and services. Identify people who are acting as producers, and provide examples of situations in which the students produced goods and services.

*At the completion of **Grade 8**, students will know the Grade 4 benchmarks for this standard and also that:*

1. Market prices are determined through the buying and selling decisions made by buyers and sellers.
2. Relative price refers to the price of one good or service compared to the prices of

other goods and services. Relative prices are the basic measures of the relative scarcity of products when prices are set by market forces (supply and demand).

3. The market clearing or equilibrium price for a good or service is the one price at which quantity supplied equals quantity demanded.

4. If a price is above the market clearing price, it will fall, causing sellers to produce less and buyers to purchase more; if it is below the market clearing price, it will rise, causing sellers to produce more and buyers to buy less.

5. An exchange rate is the price of one nation's currency in terms of another nation's currency. Like other prices, exchange rates are determined by the forces of supply and demand. Foreign exchange markets allocate international currencies.

*At the completion of **Grade 8**, students will use this knowledge to:*

1. Play a market game in which buyers and sellers determine the market price for a standardized product—for example, wheat, apples, or baseballs.

2. Explain in terms of relative scarcity why people are willing to pay higher prices for diamonds than for water, even though water is necessary for life and diamonds are not.

3. Determine the market clearing price when given a supply schedule and a demand schedule for compact discs.

4. Identify examples of products for which the price fell because sellers were unable to sell all they had produced; identify examples of other products for which the price rose because consumers wanted to buy more than producers were producing.

5. Calculate the following: (1) If the British pound is worth $1.42, how much would you have to pay in England for a compact disc that is worth $16.00? (2) If the Canadian dollar is equal to $.72 in American money, what is the Canadian equivalent of $15.00 American? (3) If it takes 1372 Italian lira to buy $1.00, how much is an Italian sweater purchased for 27,000 lira, in American dollars?

*At the completion of **Grade 12**, students will know the Grade 4 and 8 benchmarks for this standard and also that:*

1. A shortage occurs when buyers want to purchase more than producers want to sell at the prevailing price.

2. A surplus occurs when producers want to sell more than buyers want to purchase at the prevailing price.

3. Shortages of a product usually result in price increases in a market economy; surpluses usually result in price decreases.

4. When the exchange rate between two currencies changes, the relative prices of the goods and services traded among countries using those currencies change; as a result, some groups gain and others lose.

*At the completion of **Grade 12**, students will use this knowledge to:*

1. Explain why there is usually a shortage of batteries in areas where forecasters predict a hurricane and why apple bins in grocery stores are empty when disease has destroyed half of the Washington apple crop.

2. Explain why there is often a late-season surplus of tickets available for the home contests of a baseball team that loses most of its games.

3. Explain what happens (and why) to the price of tickets to sporting events purchased from scalpers when many more people want to attend those events

than the number of seats in the stadium or arena. Also, explain what will happen to the price of a rare misprinted stamp if the postal service prints another 100,000 stamps in the same way.

4. Use the following scenario to analyze the effects on trade of a change in exchange rates: In one year, the American dollar equaled 250 Japanese yen; in the following year, the American dollar equaled 150 yen; and in the third year, it equaled 200 yen. If a Nikon camera costs 75,000 yen and a Sony Walkman radio costs 25,000 yen: (1) What will be the price in dollars of these two products in each year for an American? (2) Will an American want to buy more or fewer Japanese products in year one, year two, or year three? Explain.

Content Standard 8

Students will understand that:

Prices send signals and provide incentives to buyers and sellers. When supply or demand changes, market prices adjust, affecting incentives.

Students will be able to use this knowledge to:

Predict how prices change when the number of buyers or sellers in a market changes, and explain how the incentives facing individual buyers and sellers are affected.

Understanding the role of prices as signals and incentives helps people anticipate market opportunities and make better choices as producers and consumers. It also helps citizens understand the consequences and weigh the costs and benefits of price controls, such as minimum-wage laws and rent controls, that set legal minimum or maximum prices and result in persistent surpluses or shortages.

BENCHMARKS

*At the completion of **Grade 4**, students will know that:*

1. Higher prices for a good or service provide incentives for buyers to purchase less of that good or service and for producers to make or sell more of it. Lower prices for a good or service provide incentives for buyers to purchase more of that good or service and for producers to make or sell less of it.

*At the completion of **Grade 4**, students will use this knowledge to:*

1. Predict how consumers would react if the price of pencils rose to $10 each (and explain the prediction). Predict how they would react if the price fell to $.01 each (and explain the prediction). Explain how producers would react in each situation.

*At the completion of **Grade 8**, students will know the Grade 4 benchmarks for this standard and also that:*

1. An increase in the price of a good or service encourages people to look for substitutes, causing the quantity demanded to decrease, and vice versa. This relationship between price and quantity demanded, known as the law of demand, exists

as long as other factors influencing demand do not change.

2. An increase in the price of a good or service enables producers to cover higher per-unit costs and earn profits, causing the quantity supplied to increase, and vice versa. This relationship between price and quantity supplied is normally true as long as other factors influencing costs of production and supply do not change.

3. Markets are interrelated; changes in the price of one good or service can lead to changes in prices of many other goods and services.

4. Scarce goods and services are allocated in a market economy through the influence of prices on production and consumption decisions.

At the completion of *Grade 8*, students will use this knowledge to:

1. Survey students in other classes at school regarding how many glasses of orange juice students would be willing and able to buy at various prices. Analyze the data to show the relationship between price and quantity demanded. Identify the substitutes students use when the price is higher.

2. State the number of push-ups they would be willing and able to supply at various prices. State a generalization about the relationship between price, cost, and quantity supplied from the data.

3. Explain how a decrease in the price of VCRs can cause a decrease in the price of popcorn at movie theaters.

4. Use flowcharts to illustrate the decisions of producers and consumers when the price of peanuts rises and when the price of petroleum falls, and explain why producers and consumers behave in this way.

At the completion of *Grade 12*, students will know the Grade 4 and 8 benchmarks for this standard and also that:

1. Demand for a product changes when there is a change in consumers' incomes or preferences, or in the prices of related goods or services, or in the number of consumers in a market.

2. Supply of a product changes when there are changes in the prices of the productive resources used to make the good or service, the technology used to make the good or service, the profit opportunities available to producers by selling other goods or services, or the number of sellers in a market.

3. Changes in supply or demand cause relative prices to change; in turn, buyers and sellers adjust their purchase and sales decisions.

4. Government-enforced price ceilings set below the market clearing price and government-enforced price floors set above the market clearing price distort price signals and incentives to producers and consumers. The price ceilings cause persistent shortages, while the price floors cause persistent surpluses.

At the completion of *Grade 12*, students will use this knowledge to:

1. Predict the change in demand for a particular brand of jeans when an extensive ad campaign for the brand targets teenagers, their allowances double, the price of corduroy pants skyrockets, or jeans become a popular item among adults.

2. Predict the changes in supply and market price for domestic cars when the cost of labor increases, more robotics are used to produce cars, the prices of domestic utility vehicles rise, or the number of imported cars increases.

3. Identify products that have become more or less expensive compared to other products as a result of changes in supply or demand, and explain how the price changes affected production and consumption decisions.

4. Describe what is likely to happen if the government imposes a binding price ceiling on gasoline and a binding price floor on milk.

Content Standard 9

Students will understand that:

Competition among sellers lowers costs and prices, and encourages producers to produce more of what consumers are willing and able to buy. Competition among buyers increases prices and allocates goods and services to those people who are willing and able to pay the most for them.

Students will be able to use this knowledge to:

Explain how changes in the level of competition in different markets can affect price and output levels.

Fast-food restaurants that set prices too high, or give slow, unfriendly service, risk losing customers to competing restaurants that offer lower prices, higher-quality products, and better service. In this way, competition benefits consumers. Understanding the benefits of competition and the costs of limiting competition helps students evaluate public policies that affect the level of competition in various markets. It also helps students understand their own roles as producers and consumers in a market economy—in terms of opportunities to compete with others and in terms of the limits that competition places on their incomes, career plans, and what they can buy and consume.

Competition improves productivity by forcing all suppliers to "be the best that they can be." Productivity improvements, in turn, foster economic growth and a better quality of life for current and future generations. It is important for students to recognize that competition contributes in a positive way to economic growth and the quality of life.

BENCHMARKS

At the completion of Grade 4, students will know that:
1. Competition takes place when there are many buyers and sellers of similar products.
2. Competition among sellers results in lower costs and prices, higher product quality, and better customer service.

At the completion of Grade 4, students will use this knowledge to:
1. Identify competitors in their community, using the yellow pages of the telephone book.
2. Explain how the opening of a second pizza shop in a small community affects prices, profits, service, and quality.

At the completion of Grade 8, students will know the Grade 4 benchmarks for this standard and also that:
1. Sellers compete on the basis of price, product quality, customer service, product design and variety, and advertising.

2. Competition among buyers of a product results in higher product prices.

3. The level of competition in a market is influenced by the number of buyers and sellers.

> *At the completion of **Grade 8**, students will use this knowledge to:*
>
> 1. Give examples of price and nonprice competition in the athletic shoe market.
>
> 2. Play several rounds of a market game in which the number of buyers is changed dramatically in each round, and explain the impact of these changes on price.
>
> 3. Estimate the number of producers and consumers of cereals, guided missiles, agricultural products, and electricity, and generalize about the relationship between the number of producers and consumers and the level of competition.

*At the completion of **Grade 12**, students will know the Grade 4 and 8 benchmarks for this standard and also that:*

1. The pursuit of self-interest in competitive markets generally leads to choices and behavior that also promote the national level of economic well-being.

2. The level of competition in an industry is affected by the ease with which new producers can enter the industry and by consumers' information about the availability, price, and quantity of substitute goods and services.

3. Collusion among buyers or sellers reduces the level of competition in a market. Collusion is more difficult in markets with large numbers of buyers and sellers.

4. The introduction of new products and production methods by entrepreneurs is an important form of competition, and is a source of technological progress and economic growth.

> *At the completion of **Grade 12**, students will use this knowledge to:*
>
> 1. Explain how people motivated by their own self-interest help market economies promote national well-being as long as there is active competition among buyers and sellers.
>
> 2. Explain why, in the last 10 years, there have been no U.S. companies emerging to manufacture locomotives, but many emerging to manufacture silk screen T-shirts and sports clothing. Also, predict what happened to prices of resold tickets to sporting events after Arizona required all ticket scalpers to operate only in a small roped-off area near the stadium or arena in the two hours before an event.
>
> 3. Explain why collusion is more likely to work among international airlines than among U.S. wheat farmers.
>
> 4. Create a timeline showing notable twentieth-century American entrepreneurs' products and production methods and write a brief essay on the impact of entrepreneurial activity on economic growth, competition, technological progress, and job opportunities.

Content Standard 10

Students will understand that:

Institutions evolve in market economies to help individuals and groups accomplish their goals. Banks, labor unions, corporations, legal systems, and not-for-profit organizations are examples of important institutions. A different kind of institution, clearly defined and well enforced property rights, is essential to a market economy.

Students will be able to use this knowledge to:
Describe the roles of various economic institutions.

Institutions play a number of roles in a market economy. Property rights help insure that people bear the costs and reap the benefits of their decisions. Property rights and contract enforcement encourage investment by assuring investors that they will reap the rewards of deferring consumption and assuming risk if their investments perform well. Limiting individual liability and allowing people to pool their investment resources through joint stock corporations also increases investment and future income.

Other institutions lower the costs buyers and sellers incur in their efforts to find each other in different kinds of markets. For example, banks match savers with borrowers; and investment banks match entrepreneurs who organize new firms with investors who provide the needed funds.

Many institutions work to promote the goals of certain interest groups. Labor unions, for example, increase the negotiating power of workers in their dealings with employers.

Understanding economic institutions and the purposes they serve will help students use institutions more effectively and help them evaluate proposed new institutions or changes in the existing legal and institutional environment.

BENCHMARKS

*At the completion of **Grade 4**, students will know that:*
1. Banks are institutions where people save money and earn interest, and where other people borrow money and pay interest.
2. Saving is the part of income not spent on taxes or consumption.

*At the completion of **Grade 4**, students will use this knowledge to:*
1. Explain the relationship between saving money and earning interest and borrowing money and paying interest, after participating in an activity in which they play the roles of savers and borrowers.
2. Plan a budget for an allowance. The budget will include spending for goods and services, charitable donations, sales taxes, and saving.

*At the completion of **Grade 8**, students will know the Grade 4 benchmarks for this standard and also that:*

1. Banks and other financial institutions channel funds from savers to borrowers and investors.

2. Through the process of collective bargaining with employers, labor unions represent some workers in negotiations involving wages, fringe benefits, and work rules.

3. Not-for-profit organizations are established primarily for religious, health, educational, civic, or social purposes, and they are exempt from certain taxes.

*At the completion of **Grade 8**, students will use this knowledge to:*

1. Listen to a presentation on the role banks play in channeling funds from savers to borrowers and investors and draw a diagram showing the role that financial intermediaries play among savers, borrowers, and investors.

2. Read about the establishment of the AFL-CIO; explain why it emerged and what procedures it used to gain benefits for its members.

3. Identify a not-for-profit organization and explain the rationale for its tax exemption or explain why it should not be tax exempt.

*At the completion of **Grade 12**, students will know the Grade 4 and 8 benchmarks for this standard and also that:*

1. Property rights, contract enforcement, standards for weights and measures, and liability rules affect incentives for people to produce and exchange goods and services.

2. Incorporation allows firms to accumulate sufficient financial capital to make large-scale investments and achieve economies of scale. Incorporation also reduces the risk to investors by limiting stockholders' liability to their share of ownership of the corporation.

*At the completion of **Grade 12**, students will use this knowledge to:*

1. Predict what might happen if there were no legal way to settle boundary disputes or if every state had its own system of weights and measures or currency; explain how liability for product defects affects the behavior of consumers and producers and how it affects the price of a good or service.

2. Play the role of a business consultant hired to advise a partnership on the advantages it could enjoy by incorporating; write a letter outlining these benefits for their client.

Content Standard 11

Students will understand that:

Money makes it easier to trade, borrow, save, invest, and compare the value of goods and services.

Students will be able to use this knowledge to:

Explain how their lives would be more difficult in a world with no money or in a world where money sharply lost its value.

Most people would like to have more money. Students, however, often fail to understand that the real value of money is determined by the goods and services money can buy. Doubling the amount of money in an economy overnight would not, by itself, make people better off, because there would still be the same amount of goods and services produced and consumed, only at higher prices. Money is important to an economy, however, because as it replaces barter it makes exchange less costly. As a result, people are more likely to specialize in what they produce, using money to buy what they want to consume, thus increasing overall levels of production and consumption in a nation.

Understanding what determines the real buying power of money and earnings will help students make better decisions about their jobs and spending. Understanding the importance of money to society will also help them make informed decisions about national policies related to banking, controlling the supply of money, and inflation.

BENCHMARKS

*At the completion of **Grade 4**, students will know that:*

1. Money is anything widely accepted as final payment for goods and services.
2. Money makes trading easier by replacing barter with transactions involving currency, coins, or checks.
3. People consume goods and services, not money; money is useful primarily because it can be used to buy goods and services.
4. Producers use natural resources, human resources, and capital goods (not money) to make goods and services.
5. Most countries create their own currency for use as money.

*At the completion of **Grade 4**, students will use this knowledge to:*

1. Identify things that have been used as money at different times and in different societies. Explain why some things can be used effectively for money and some things cannot.
2. List five goods and services they desire and describe ways of obtaining these goods and services without using money. Then explain why using money makes it easier to get the same five items.
3. Decide whether they would rather have a suitcase full of money or one full of food when stranded on a deserted island, and explain their answer.
4. Explain why, when given money, they are unable to produce paper weights to sell at the forthcoming school craft fair unless they exchange the money for productive resources.
5. Identify the currencies they would want to buy if they were going on a trip to Brazil, France, Romania, Vietnam, Australia, Japan, and Kenya.

*At the completion of **Grade 8**, students will know the Grade 4 benchmarks for this standard and also that:*

1. As a store of value, money makes it easier for people to save and defer consumption until the future.
2. As a unit of account, money is used to compare the market value of different goods and services.
3. Money encourages specialization by decreasing the costs of exchange.

*At the completion of **Grade 8**, students will use this knowledge to:*

1. Demonstrate their understanding of money as a store of value in responding to the following: A tomato farmer wants to save money for his five-year-old daughter's college education. Why is he better off selling his tomatoes for money and saving the money than he would be if he saved tomatoes to exchange for his daughter's tuition when she reaches age 18?

2. Explain how they can use relative prices to compare the value of three different fruits.

3. Explain how life might change for Dr. Hart, who specializes as a cardiologist, and for others in the community, if our society became a barter economy.

*At the completion of **Grade 12**, students will know the Grade 4 and 8 benchmarks for this standard and also that:*

1. The basic money supply in the United States consists of currency, coins, and checking account deposits.

2. In many economies, when banks make loans, the money supply increases; when loans are paid off, the money supply decreases.

*At the completion of **Grade 12**, students will use this knowledge to:*

1. Select examples of money from a collection of pictures that show coins, currency, checks, savings account passbooks, ATM cards, and various types of credit cards and explain whether each is considered money.

2. Demonstrate how successive deposits and loans by commercial banks, resulting from one new deposit in the banking system, cause the money supply to expand and how repayment of loans causes the money supply to contract.

Content Standard 12

Students will understand that:

Interest rates, adjusted for inflation, rise and fall to balance the amount saved with the amount borrowed, thus affecting the allocation of scarce resources between present and future uses.

Students will be able to use this knowledge to:

Explain situations in which they pay or receive interest, and explain how they would react to changes in interest rates if they were making or receiving interest payments.

Interest rates influence the borrowing and saving of business investors, consumers, and government agencies. Most people are unfamiliar with interest rates until they borrow money for a major purchase such as an automobile, college education, or a house. When they enter the market for credit they encounter an unfamiliar price (the interest rate) offered by an unfamiliar business (a financial institution). It is necessary for students to understand that interest rates are determined by market forces that balance savings and borrowing. For many people, interest rates can represent significant financial costs and significant financial benefits over a lifetime.

It is also important for students to understand the incentive effects of interest rates. Interest payments compensate savers for postponing current consumption; they compensate lenders for the risk that borrowers might default on their loans; and they cover the cost of expected inflation over the term of the loan.

BENCHMARKS

*At the completion of **Grade 12**, students will know that:*

1. An interest rate is a price of money that is borrowed or saved.

2. Like other prices, interest rates are determined by the forces of supply and demand.

3. The real interest rate is the nominal or current market interest rate minus the expected rate of inflation.

4. Higher real interest rates provide incentives for people to save more and to borrow less. Lower real interest rates provide incentives for people to save less and to borrow more.

5. Real interest rates normally are positive because people must be compensated for deferring the use of resources from the present into the future.

6. Riskier loans command higher interest rates than safer loans because of the greater chance of default on the repayment of risky loans.

7. Higher interest rates reduce business investment spending and consumer spending on housing, cars, and other major purchases. Policies that raise interest rates can be used to reduce these kinds of spending, while policies that decrease interest rates can be used to increase these kinds of spending.

*At the completion of **Grade 12**, students will use this knowledge to:*

1. Identify the current rates of interest on different kinds of savings instruments and different kinds of loans.

2. Determine the interest rates on 30-year fixed-rate conventional home mortgages over the last 15 years and explain why they rose and fell.

3. Collect data on the inflation and interest rates for various kinds of loans and savings instruments over the past 15 years. Discuss the relationship between the observed inflation rates and expected rates of inflation in any given year. Using this information, estimate the real rate of interest in these different years.

4. Collect data on interest rates, inflation rates, and new housing starts over the past 25 years. State how changes in real interest rates affect people's decisions to borrow in order to buy a house.

5. Explain why people who save money receive interest payments while people who borrow money make interest payments.

6. Explain why there are usually differences in interest rates for new and used-car loans, for 15-year versus 30-year mortgages, and for individuals with good and bad credit ratings.

7. Identify periods over the past 10 years when the Federal Reserve System tried to increase interest rates in order to reduce business, investment, and consumer spending.

Content Standard 13

Students will understand that:

Income for most people is determined by the market value of the productive resources they sell. What workers earn depends, primarily, on the market value of what they produce and how productive they are.

Students will be able to use this knowledge to:

Predict future earnings based on their current plans for education, training, and career options.

In a market economy, wages and salaries—the prices of labor services—are determined just as other prices are, by the interaction of buyers and sellers. The buyers of labor services are employers. They are willing to pay higher wages and salaries to employees who can produce more or better goods or services in a given amount of time. Students who understand this will appreciate the value of the skills they can acquire by completing high school, and perhaps college or a vocational training program.

Understanding the forces affecting wages and other sources of income will be increasingly important in the future, when workers may change employers and careers more often than in the past. Regardless of the occupations or industries in which today's students eventually work, they are likely to find that they will have to continue their education and training to maintain or increase their earnings.

BENCHMARKS

*At the completion of **Grade 4**, students will know that:*
1. Labor is a human resource used to produce goods and services.
2. People can earn income by exchanging their human resources (physical or mental work) for wages or salaries.

*At the completion of **Grade 4**, students will use this knowledge to:*
1. Identify human resources in their community and the goods and services they produce.
2. Collect data from adults regarding their reasons for working, analyze the data, and generalize about why people work.

*At the completion of **Grade 8**, students will know the Grade 4 benchmarks for this standard and also that:*
1. Employers are willing to pay wages and salaries to workers because they expect to sell the goods and services those workers produce at prices high enough to cover the wages and salaries and all other costs of production.
2. To earn income, people sell productive resources. These include their labor, capital, natural resources, and entrepreneurial talents.
3. A wage or salary is the price of labor; it usually is determined by the supply of and demand for labor.

4. More productive workers are likely to be of greater value to employers and earn higher wages than less productive workers.

5. People's incomes, in part, reflect choices they have made about education, training, skill development, and careers. People with few skills are more likely to be poor.

*At the completion of **Grade 8**, students will use this knowledge to:*

1. Ask owners of fast-food restaurants why they are willing to pay a wage or salary to workers and conclude that restaurant owners do so because they expect to sell the food and services produced at a price high enough to cover the wages, salaries, and all other costs of production.

2. Survey several adults regarding their sources of income, and conclude that the largest portion of personal income for most people comes from wages and salaries.

3. Participate in a market simulation as employers and employees to determine wage rates for labor.

4. Decide which workers to hire and explain the hiring decisions, given a list of job applicants with different levels of productivity.

5. Consider a career choice and research the amount of education required and the median income for this career. Identify reasons why high school dropouts frequently earn low incomes.

*At the completion of **Grade 12**, students will know the Grade 4 and 8 benchmarks for this standard and also that:*

1. Changes in the structure of the economy, the level of gross domestic product, technology, government policies, and discrimination can influence personal income.

2. In a labor market, in the absence of other changes, if wage or salary payments increase, workers will increase the quantity of labor they supply and firms will decrease the quantity of labor they demand.

3. Changes in the prices for productive resources affect the incomes of the owners of those productive resources and the combination of those resources used by firms.

4. Changes in demand for specific goods and services often affect the incomes of the workers who make those goods and services.

5. Two methods for classifying how income is distributed in a nation—the personal distribution of income and the functional distribution—reflect, respectively, the distribution of income among different groups of households and the distribution of income among different businesses and occupations in the economy.

*At the completion of **Grade 12**, students will use this knowledge to:*

1. Review income data for jobs in manufacturing and service industries over the last 25 years. Explain how changes in the structure of the economy, gross domestic product, technology, government, prices, and discrimination have influenced income for jobs in these two areas.

2. Explain the impact of an increase in the minimum wage on their ability to secure an after-school job; also explain the impact of the increase on their willingness to work.

3. Construct a flow chart to show how a change in a resource price affects producers and workers in a particular production process.

4. List three careers that are expected to provide many new job openings and explain why. List three careers that are expected to experience a decline in job openings and explain why.

5. Identify the major changes in the functional distribution of income in the United States between the 1780s and the 1990s. Also, determine whether there have been significant changes in the personal income distribution in the United States over the past 50 years.

Content Standard 14

Students will understand that:

Entrepreneurs are people who take the risks of organizing productive resources to make goods and services. Profit is an important incentive that leads entrepreneurs to accept the risks of business failure.

Students will be able to use this knowledge to:

Identify the risks, returns, and other characteristics of entrepreneurship that bear on its attractiveness as a career.

Starting a new business, such as a "drive thru" that sells fruit-freezes, is difficult and risky. Challenges abound: hiring and managing the workers to make and serve the freezes, ordering supplies and making sure they arrive on time, giving prompt and courteous service so customers will return, and earning enough money to pay workers, taxes, suppliers, and everyone else involved in the production and sales process, while still leaving something for the owner.

Spending money and using resources to supply a product is risky because costs are incurred before consumers decide whether they will purchase the product at a price sufficiently high to cover the costs. Starting a new business or producing an entirely new product is especially risky because in the case of a new product producers know even less about how consumers will react. Entrepreneurs accept the risks and organize productive resources to get products produced. Profits are the financial incentive and the income that entrepreneurs receive in return for their effort and risk—*if* they are successful. If they are not successful, losses are the financial incentives that tell entrepreneurs to stop using resources as they have been using them.

Understanding the roles of entrepreneurs, profits, and losses is important to workers, business owners, and consumers. Wages and employment opportunities at a business depend on the business's success in earning profits and avoiding losses. Similarly, public policies that affect the profitability of a business will influence not only the owners and employees of the business, but also the consumers who buy the products produced by the business.

BENCHMARKS

*At the completion of **Grade 4**, students will know that:*

1. Entrepreneurs are individuals who are willing to take risks in order to develop new products and start new businesses. They recognize opportunities, enjoy working for themselves, and accept challenges.

2. An invention is a new product. Innovation is the introduction of an invention into a use that has economic value.

3. Entrepreneurs often are innovative. They attempt to solve problems by developing and marketing new or improved products.

*At the completion of **Grade 4**, students will use this knowledge to:*

1. Read a children's book about an entrepreneur. Identify the main character's entrepreneurial characteristics and compare their own entrepreneurial characteristics with those of the main character.

2. Identify three examples of inventions and three examples of innovations.

3. Solve a problem by creating a new use for an existing product such as a wire coat hanger, thimble, or shoulder pad. Also, develop an advertising campaign for their new product.

*At the completion of **Grade 8**, students will know the Grade 4 benchmarks for this standard and also that:*

1. Entrepreneurs compare the expected benefits of entering a new enterprise with the expected costs.

2. Entrepreneurs accept the risks in organizing resources to produce goods and services, and they hope to earn profits.

3. Entrepreneurs and other sellers earn profits when buyers purchase the products they sell at prices high enough to cover the costs of production.

4. Entrepreneurs and other sellers incur losses when buyers do not purchase the products they sell at prices high enough to cover the costs of production.

5. In addition to profits, entrepreneurs respond to other incentives including the opportunity to be their own boss, the chance to achieve recognition, and the satisfaction of creating new products or improving existing ones. In addition to financial losses, other disincentives to which entrepreneurs respond include the responsibility, long hours, and stress of running a business.

*At the completion of **Grade 8**, students will use this knowledge to:*

1. Read short biographies of various entrepreneurs and identify the risks each entrepreneur faced and the entrepreneur's incentive(s) for accepting the risk.

2. Interview an entrepreneur to learn why he or she was willing to start a new business.

3. Analyze simple profit and loss statements and conclude that entrepreneurs or other sellers earn profits when their total revenues exceed their total costs.

4. Identify a restaurant that went out of business and give reasons why this might have occurred.

5. Read short biographies of several entrepreneurs, list the pertinent characteristics of each entrepreneur, and make a generalization about the non-financial incentives that motivate entrepreneurs and the risks or disincentives entrepreneurs face.

*At the completion of **Grade 12**, students will know the Grade 4 and 8 benchmarks for this standard and also that:*

1. Entrepreneurial decisions affect job opportunities for other workers.

2. Entrepreneurial decisions are influenced by government tax and regulatory policies.

*At the completion of **Grade 12**, students will use this knowledge to:*
1. Identify an entrepreneur and describe how the entrepreneur's decisions affect job opportunities.
2. Explain how entrepreneurial activity is affected by a tax policy that affects income from profits and capital investment.

Content Standard 15

Students will understand that:

Investment in factories, machinery, new technology, and the health, education, and training of people can raise future standards of living.

Students will be able to use this knowledge to:

Predict the consequences of investment decisions made by individuals, businesses, and governments.

Students should recognize that by saving and investing money today they can benefit in the future by being able to buy such things as a car, a compact disc player, a trip to an amusement park, or other things that cost more than they can afford immediately. They will face similar trade-offs throughout their lives. As adults they will save for many things other than toys and vacations—including housing, medical expenses, taxes, household and automobile repairs, their children's education, and their own retirement. Savings deposited in banks and other financial institutions earn interest because those savings are loaned to business people who want to invest in capital goods, or to people who are willing to pay higher interest rates to purchase homes, cars, or other things now rather than later. The new physical capital will, in turn, increase production and promote faster economic growth.

Businesses, governments, and other organizations face decisions similar to those confronting individuals: future benefits that arise from saving and investing today make it worthwhile to sacrifice some current spending. Knowing this will help students understand the various investment and dividend programs adopted by different corporations, as well as public policies involving taxation, spending programs, and investment in infrastructure, education, and other things that will increase future standards of living. It will help them appreciate that a better life in the future often requires patience and sacrifice in the present. It also will help them understand the importance of personal investment in education and training, and of business investments.

BENCHMARKS

*At the completion of **Grade 4**, students will know that:*
1. When workers learn and practice new skills they are improving their human capital.
2. Workers can improve their productivity by improving their human capital.
3. Workers can improve their productivity by using physical capital such as tools and machinery.

*At the completion of **Grade 4**, students will use this knowledge to:*
1. Explain why professional athletes often have training equipment in their homes.

2. Make a pressman's hat out of newspaper with no instructions, record how much time it took to make the hat, and discuss the quality of the finished product. After receiving instruction on how to make the hat, and given time to practice, repeat the activity, record how long it takes to make the hat, and compare the quality of the hats produced with and without instructions and practice.

3. Complete a basic math worksheet using pencil and paper in a given amount of time; correct the work and record the number of problems completed and the number of correct answers. Repeat the activity, using calculators; correct the work, record the number of problems completed and the number of correct answers, and explain the difference in results.

*At the completion of **Grade 8**, students will know the Grade 4 benchmarks for this standard and also that:*

1. Standards of living increase as the productivity of labor improves.

2. Productivity is measured by dividing output (goods and services) by the number of inputs used to produce the output. A change in productivity is a change in output relative to input.

3. Technological change is an advance in knowledge leading to new and improved goods and services and better ways of producing them.

4. Increases in productivity result from advances in technology and other sources.

*At the completion of **Grade 8**, students will use this knowledge to:*

1. Analyze data on labor productivity and standards of living. Draw a generalization about the relationship between the two. Also, tell how the living standards of their families would probably change if the productivity of every worker in the United States were to increase by 20 percent.

2. Participate in a simulated production process in which they calculate productivity and analyze changes that occur through investment in human capital and capital goods.

3. Create a timeline showing at least five new products that have been developed over the last 25 years. Also, explain how technological change led to these new or improved products.

4. Study data about technological development and labor productivity for the last 25 years in the United States, India, Haiti, and Germany. Generalize about the relationship between technological change and changes in productivity from the data.

*At the completion of **Grade 12**, students will know the Grade 4 and 8 benchmarks for this standard and also that:*

1. Economic growth is a sustained rise in a nation's production of goods and services. It results from investments in human and physical capital, research and development, technological change, and improved institutional arrangements and incentives.

2. Historically, economic growth has been the primary vehicle for alleviating poverty and raising standards of living.

3. Economic growth creates new employment and profit opportunities in some industries, but growth reduces opportunities in others.

4. Investments in physical and human capital can increase productivity, but such investments entail opportunity costs and economic risks.

5. Investing in new physical or human capital involves a trade-off of lower current consumption in anticipation of greater future production and consumption.

6. Higher interest rates discourage investment.

7. The rate of productivity increase in an economy is strongly affected by the incentives that reward successful innovation and investments (in research and development, and in physical and human capital).

*At the completion of **Grade 12**, students will use this knowledge to:*

1. Analyze per capita real GDP data for several periods in history, identifying periods during which the United States experienced rapid economic growth; identify the factors that contributed to this growth.

2. Compare the material standard of living of individuals living in the United States in 1790, 1890, and 1990; explain the relationship between higher productivity levels, new technologies, and the standard of living.

3. Tell how growth in the computer industry affects employment and profit opportunities in the computer industry and in the typewriter industry.

4. Engage in a simulated production activity involving investment in human capital and capital goods and identify the effect on productivity as well as the opportunity costs and economic risks.

5. Discuss the advantages and disadvantages of investing in a riding mower, given the following information: A teenager mows lawns to earn income. If she purchases a riding mower, she can mow more lawns in less time and possibly earn more income.

6. Explain why the purchase of an old car to use for delivering pizzas is less attractive when interest rates are higher.

7. Explain how copyrights in the popular music industry and patents in the pharmaceutical industry affect the rate of productivity in each industry.

Content Standard 16

Students will understand that:

There is an economic role for government to play in a market economy whenever the benefits of a government policy outweigh its costs. Governments often provide for national defense, address environmental concerns, define and protect property rights, and attempt to make markets more competitive. Most government policies also redistribute income.

Students will be able to use this knowledge to:

Identify and evaluate the benefits and costs of alternative public policies, and assess who enjoys the benefits and who bears the costs.

Why does the government pay private construction firms to build roads and highways? Why do the firms that build the roads not own them themselves and charge tolls to users? All kinds of goods and services are produced and distributed through private markets, so why not roads and highways, too? In flipping through the pages of the telephone directory, we observe a vast array of businesses and government agencies. Why do markets work well to supply much of what we want, while failing to produce other things we want?

Citizens should understand the limitations and shortcomings of markets and how some government policies attempt to compensate for market failures. Learning the economic as well as the political and social reasons for public sector services helps citizens make better choices about the appropriate size and scope of markets and government. It is also important that students be able to evaluate redistributive effects of government programs.

BENCHMARKS

*At the completion of **Grade 4**, students will know that:*
1. Governments provide certain kinds of goods and services in a market economy.
2. Governments pay for the goods and services they use or provide by taxing or borrowing from people.

*At the completion of **Grade 4**, students will use this knowledge to:*
1. Brainstorm a list of goods and services not privately produced and explain how these goods and services are paid for.
2. Apply knowledge of the role of government in the economy in responding to the following questions: Your community wants a new bridge. Who will pay for this bridge and how will they get the money? Why is this the best way to pay for bridges?

*At the completion of **Grade 8**, students will know the Grade 4 benchmarks for this standard and also that:*
1. Public goods and services provide benefits to more than one person at the same time, and their use cannot be restricted only to those people who have paid to use them.
2. If a good or service cannot be withheld from those who do not pay for it, providers expect to be unable to sell it and therefore will not produce it. In market economies, governments provide some of these goods and services.
3. In the United States, the federal government enforces antitrust laws and regulations to try to maintain effective levels of competition in as many markets as possible; frequently, however, laws and regulations also have unintended effects—for example, reducing competition.
4. Most federal tax revenue comes from personal income and payroll taxes. Payments to social security recipients, the costs of national defense, medical expenditures, and interest payments on the national debt constitute the bulk of federal government spending.
5. Most state and local government revenues come from sales taxes, grants from the federal government, personal income taxes, and property taxes. The bulk of state and local government revenue is spent for education, public welfare, road construction and repair, and public safety.

*At the completion of **Grade 8**, students will use this knowledge to:*
1. Explain why tax dollars are used to pay for national defense, elementary school education, and roads. Explain why, without government, these services would be underprovided in the private sector?
2. Answer the following question: If the national, state, and local governments had no power to tax, what goods and services would we have to do without?

3. Explain why the Federal Trade Commission might prevent the purchase of one large corporation by its closest competitor and what the effects might be on consumers, producers, and workers if the sale were allowed.

4. Use data from the U.S. federal budget to construct two pie charts—one representing major categories of federal revenue and one representing major categories of federal expenditures.

5. Compare the various sources of state and local revenues and various categories of state and local expenditures in their state and community with those for the U.S. federal government.

*At the completion of **Grade 12**, students will know the Grade 4 and 8 benchmarks for this standard and also that:*

1. Markets do not allocate resources effectively if (1) property rights are not clearly defined or enforced, (2) externalities (spillover effects) affecting large numbers of people are associated with the production or consumption of a product, or (3) markets are not competitive.

2. An important role for government in the economy is to define, establish, and enforce property rights. A property right to a good or service includes the right to exclude others from using the good or service and the right to transfer the ownership or use of the resource to others.

3. Property rights provide incentives for the owners of resources to weigh the value of present uses against the value of conserving the resources for future use.

4. Externalities exist when some of the costs and benefits associated with production and consumption fall on someone other than the producers or consumers of the product.

5. When a price fails to reflect all the benefits of a product, too little of the product is produced and consumed. When a price fails to reflect all the costs of a product, too much of it is produced and consumed. Government can use subsidies to help correct for insufficient output; it can use taxes to help correct for excessive output; or it can regulate output directly to correct for over- or under-production or consumption of a product.

6. When one producer can supply total output in a market at a cost that is lower than the cost incurred when two or more producers divide production, competition may be impossible. In the absence of competition, government regulations may then be used to try to control price, output, and quality.

7. Governments often redistribute income directly when individuals or interest groups are not satisfied with the income distribution resulting from markets; governments also redistribute income indirectly as side-effects of other government actions that affect prices or output levels for various goods and services.

8. Governments provide an alternative method to markets for supplying goods and services when it appears that the benefits to society of doing so outweigh the costs to society. Not all individuals will bear the same costs or share the same benefits of those policies.

9. A government policy to correct a market imperfection is not justified economically if its expected costs exceed its expected benefits.

*At the completion of **Grade 12**, students will use this knowledge to:*

1. Identify at least three economic roles of the U.S. federal government and cite a specific example of each.

2. Predict what would happen to some land they own if they had no right to restrict its use by others or if they found crude oil on this land but had no right to sell the oil.

3. Analyze the following scenario and predict probable economic and social consequences: To save money, Congress passes, and the President signs into law, a bill that makes it illegal for any government to settle disputes over property rights. From now on, property-related disputes will be settled privately.

4. Explain why there is a role for government in dealing with pollution, vaccinations, and medical research; recommend what this role should be.

5. Explain why state and local governments use public money to pay for elementary education and why tobacco and gasoline are heavily taxed.

6. Explain why there is usually only one local water and sewer supplier.

7. Describe three government assistance programs, explain why government provides them, and determine which groups in the economy benefit from them and which groups bear the costs to fund them.

8. Discuss the costs and benefits of public education and identify who gains the most and who bears most of these costs.

9. Analyze the costs and benefits of a $500 per person state government job-training program to help adults without jobs. Make a recommendation on whether or not implementing this program is a good economic decision.

Content Standard 17

Students will understand that:

Costs of government policies sometimes exceed benefits. This may occur because of incentives facing voters, government officials, and government employees, because of actions by special interest groups that can impose costs on the general public, or because social goals other than economic efficiency are being pursued.

Students will be able to use this knowledge to:

Identify some public policies that may cost more than the benefits they generate, and assess who enjoys the benefits and who bears the costs. Explain why the policies exist.

Do government officials try to promote the general welfare of the nation, or are they guided by their own self-interests? Businesses that fail to satisfy consumer wants go bankrupt; but how do we know when government programs fail, and how do we change or eliminate failed government programs? Why do some farmers receive large subsidies from the government, and why are many businesses protected from competition by tariffs or quotas—even when only a small percentage of the U.S. labor force is employed in those industries? Why don't taxpayers rise up and put a stop to the favoritism accorded to certain industries and special interest groups? And why do so few people participate in the political process, and so many choose not to register or vote?

It is important to realize that governments, like markets, also have shortcomings and imperfections. Citizens should understand the sources of these imperfections, including the distribution of costs and benefits of some programs that lead to special-interest problems, the costs involved in gathering and using information about different candidates and government programs, and the incentives that can induce government leaders and employees to act in ways that do not promote the general national interest. Understanding this allows citizens to compare actual with ideal government performance, and to decide about the appropriate roles for federal, state, and local government.

BENCHMARKS

*At the completion of **Grade 12**, students will know that:*

1. Citizens, government employees, and elected officials do not always directly bear the costs of their political decisions. This often leads to policies whose costs outweigh their benefits for society.

2. Incentives exist for political leaders to implement policies that disperse costs widely over large groups of people and benefit relatively small, politically powerful groups of people.

3. Incentives exist for political leaders to favor programs that entail immediate benefits and deferred costs; few incentives favor programs promising immediate costs and deferred benefits, even though the latter programs are sometimes economically more effective than the former programs.

4. Although barriers to international trade usually impose more costs than benefits, they are often advocated by people and groups who expect to gain substantially from them. Because the costs of these barriers are typically spread over a large number of people who each pay only a little and may not recognize the cost, policies supporting trade barriers are often adopted through the political process.

5. Price controls are often advocated by special interest groups. Price controls reduce the quantity of goods and services consumed, thus depriving consumers of some goods and services whose value would exceed their cost.

*At the Completion of **Grade 12**, students will use this knowledge to:*

1. Predict the costs that would be imposed on the public if federal taxes were reduced and the budget were balanced by Congress, and explain how political goals may conflict with economic goals.

2. Explain why a political leader would support an idea that helps only a few while harming many, such as a tariff on imported luggage or an import quota on sugar.

3. Explain why, although most Americans say they are in favor of reducing the deficit, Congress does not vote to increase taxes.

4. Analyze the following scenario: The United States allows Taiwan to export shirts to this country without placing a tariff on the imports. The Taiwanese can produce shirts at half the cost of shirts produced by American manufacturers. What groups in the United States and Taiwan will be helped, and what groups will be hurt, if the United States continues the present free-trade policy toward Taiwan? Prepare an argument supporting the American shirt manufacturers' desire for a tariff on Taiwanese shirts.

5. Explain the following statement: *Removing rent controls in New York City is good economics but bad politics.* Also, explain who would gain and who would lose as a result of a 10 percent ceiling on credit card interest rates.

Content Standard 18

Students will understand that:

A nation's overall levels of income, employment, and prices are determined by the interaction of spending and production decisions made by all households, firms, government agencies, and others in the economy.

Students will be able to use this knowledge to:

Interpret media reports about current economic conditions and explain how these conditions can influence decisions made by consumers, producers, and government policymakers.

Changes in national levels of spending, production, and income can seem rather abstract and remote to students, because individuals can do little or nothing to change overall levels of economic activity. But these activity levels can have a profound effect on students' future welfare, their job opportunities, the level of their prospective earnings, and the prices they will pay for things they buy. It is important, therefore, for students to understand possible causes of changes in these levels and how such changes can produce problems (such as unemployment and inflation) or opportunities (such as increased employment). Understanding these macroeconomic forces equips students to anticipate and respond intelligently to economic developments. It also enables students to predict the economic consequences of proposed government policies and to make informed choices among alternative political candidates and public policy proposals.

BENCHMARKS

*At the completion of **Grade 8**, students will know that:*

1. Gross Domestic Product (GDP) is a basic measure of a nation's economic output and income. It is the total market value, measured in dollars, of all final goods and services produced in the economy in one year.
2. Per capita GDP is GDP divided by the number of people living in a country.
3. When consumers make purchases, goods and services are transferred from businesses to households in exchange for money payments. That money is used in turn by businesses to pay for productive resources (natural, human, and capital) and to pay taxes.

*At the completion of **Grade 8**, students will use this knowledge to:*

1. Explain what GDP is and how it can be used to describe a country's economic output over time, comparing outputs from year to year.
2. Determine the per capita GDP for several countries, given data on population and GDP for each country. Identify a few other countries whose per capita GDP is similar to that of the United States.
3. Draw and label a circular flow diagram and explain the interrelated roles of households, businesses, and government in the economy.

*At the completion of **Grade 12**, students will know the Grade 8 benchmarks for this standard and also that:*

1. Nominal GDP is measured in current dollars; thus, an increase in GDP may reflect not only increases in the production of goods and services, but also increases in prices. GDP adjusted for price changes is called real GDP. Real GDP per capita is a measure that permits comparisons of material living standards over time and among people in different nations.

2. The potential level of real GDP for a nation is determined by the quantity and quality of its natural resources, the size and skills of its labor force, and the size and quality of its stock of capital resources.

3. One person's spending is other people's income. Consequently, an initial change in spending (consumption, investment, government, or net exports) usually results in a larger change in national levels of income, spending, and output.

4. When desired expenditures for consumption, investment, government spending, and net exports are greater than the value of a nation's output of final goods and services, GDP rises and inflation occurs and/or employment rises.

5. When desired expenditures for consumption, investment, government spending, and net exports are less than the value of a nation's output of final goods and services, GDP decreases and inflation and/or employment decreases.

*At the completion of **Grade 12**, students will use this knowledge to:*

1. Gather current and historical data on real GDP per capita for the United States, Japan, Somalia, and South Korea and state a relationship between real GDP and standard of living.

2. Locate and analyze relevant data from appropriate reference materials to assess the validity of the following statement: *It is doubtful that many of the countries of Sub-Saharan Africa will ever have GDPs that approach the value of those of Western European countries.*

3. Read the following scenario and analyze the effects on the economy: A visitor comes into a community and spends $100 on a single purchase at a video store. The video store's income increases by $100. It spends $80 of the money to pay the telephone bill, which now becomes income to the telephone company, and so forth.

4. Describe the effect on the economy when desired expenditures for consumption, investment, government spending, and net exports exceed the value of a nation's output of final goods and services.

5. Describe the effect on the economy when desired expenditures for consumption, investment, government spending, and net exports are less than the value of a nation's output of final goods and services.

Content Standard 19

Students will understand that:

Unemployment imposes costs on individuals and nations. Unexpected inflation imposes costs on many people and benefits some others because it arbitrarily redistributes purchasing power. Inflation can reduce the rate of growth of national living standards, because individuals and organizations use resources to protect themselves against the uncertainty of future prices.

Students will be able to use this knowledge to:

Make informed decisions by anticipating the consequences of inflation and unemployment.

Inflation and unemployment are important because they affect national levels of economic growth and standards of living. Some aspects of inflation and unemployment can be addressed with public policies. Various political leaders and parties often have different ideas about which policies should be followed to deal with inflation and unemployment, however. The controversial policies, and the fact that almost everyone is affected by unemployment or inflation, explain why these two problems and alternative approaches to combat them are so widely reported in the news media, and why understanding them is important to citizens in a democratic political system.

BENCHMARKS

*At the completion of **Grade 4**, students will know that:*

1. Inflation is an increase in most prices; deflation is a decrease in most prices.
2. Unemployment exists when people who are actively looking for work do not have jobs.

*At the completion of **Grade 4**, students will use this knowledge to:*

1. Determine in which years inflation occurred and in which years deflation occurred, given the prices for a market basket of goods and services for three different years.
2. Apply the standard definition of an unemployed person by explaining why retired people and students are not considered unemployed.

*At the completion of **Grade 8**, students will know the Grade 4 benchmarks for this standard and also that:*

1. When unemployment exists, an economy's production is less than potential GDP and some labor resources are not used.
2. The labor force consists of people aged 16 and over who are employed or actively seeking work.
3. Inflation reduces the value of money.
4. When people's incomes increase more slowly than the inflation rate, their purchasing power declines.

*At the completion of **Grade 8**, students will use this knowledge to:*

1. Identify goods or services that could be produced if the local community's unemployed had jobs. Draw a flow chart that shows a ripple effect resulting from unemployment in a particular industry or community.
2. Determine whether each of the following is counted as a member of the labor force: (1) an elementary school student who has a paper route; (2) an army captain; (3) a retired butcher; (4) an insurance salesperson; (5) a woman who has decided not to work outside the home until her children are in school; and (6) a 42-year-old civil engineer who looked for a job for two years, but finally gave up searching when he could not find work in that field.
3. Interview someone 50-59 years old. Ask about grocery prices. Compare the

groceries that could be purchased for $10 in 1967 with those that can be purchased for $10 today.

4. Compare the prices of a market basket of goods in 1980 with similar prices today. Explain how inflation reduces purchasing power for people whose income is either fixed or increasing slower than the rate of inflation.

*At the completion of **Grade 12**, students will know the Grade 4 and 8 benchmarks for this standard and also that:*

1. The unemployment rate is the percentage of the labor force that is willing and able to work, does not currently have a job, and is actively looking for work.

2. The unemployment rate is an imperfect measure of unemployment because it does not (1) include workers whose job prospects are so poor that they are discouraged from seeking jobs, or (2) reflect part-time workers who are looking for full-time work.

3. Unemployment rates differ for people of different ages, races, and sexes. This reflects differences in work experience, education, training, and skills, as well as discrimination.

4. Unemployment can be caused by people changing jobs, by seasonal fluctuations in demand, by changes in the skills needed by employers, or by cyclical fluctuations in the level of national spending.

5. Full employment means that the only unemployed people in the economy are those who are changing jobs.

6. The consumer price index (CPI) is the most commonly used measure of price-level changes. It can be used to compare the price level in one year with price levels in earlier or later periods.

7. Expectations of increased inflation may lead to higher interest rates.

8. The costs of inflation are different for different groups of people. Unexpected inflation hurts savers and people on fixed incomes; it helps people who have borrowed money at a fixed rate of interest.

9. Inflation imposes costs on people beyond its effects on wealth distribution because people devote resources to protect themselves from expected inflation.

*At the completion of **Grade 12**, students will use this knowledge to:*

1. Calculate the unemployment rate for the following situation: Berks County has 200,000 people. Of that population, 70,000 are full-time housewives, students, children, retired people, or people not looking for work. Of the remaining residents of Berks County, 110,000 people have jobs.

2. Explain why the following may be true: A weekly news magazine reports that the current unemployment statistic does not accurately reflect the true impact of unemployment.

3. Locate data pertaining to unemployment rates for young people and minorities, and explain why unemployment rates for these groups differ from the unemployment rates for other groups in the economy.

4. Give examples of each type of unemployment, analyze the differences among them, and identify which types cause more serious problems in the economy.

5. Explain why some people are unemployed when the economy is said to be functioning at full employment.

6. Determine the current price for a pair of designer sunglasses that cost $50 in 1982, assuming the price has increased at the average rate of inflation.

7. Explain their answer to the following question: If you were going to lend $100 to someone for a year, would you ask for more or less interest if you expected the prices of most things you buy to rise substantially over the year?

8. For each of the following cases, tell who would be harmed by an unexpected 10 percent inflation rate, who would benefit, and explain why: (1) Mike's retirement income is $24,000 a year; (2) Liany borrowed $5,000 last year and must pay it back at the end of this year; (3) John lent the $5,000 to Liany last year and will be paid back at the end of this year; (4) Bob and Monika bought several houses as an investment 10 years ago, and now they plan to sell them; and (5) businesses sell consumer products such as clothing and food.

9. Identify assets people can buy to protect themselves financially against inflation and discuss how much time people spend with this problem in times of high inflation (e.g., 1981) compared to times of low inflation (e.g. 1955).

Content Standard 20

Students will understand that:

Federal government budgetary policy and the Federal Reserve System's monetary policy influence the overall levels of employment, output, and prices.

Students will be able to use this knowledge to:

Anticipate the impact of the federal government's and the Federal Reserve System's macroeconomic policy decisions on themselves and others.

The U.S. federal government's taxation and spending policies and the Federal Reserve System's monetary policies affect the nation's overall levels of employment, output, and prices. However, many government taxation and spending activities are undertaken for other reasons, as well. Government expenditures for national defense, human services, and other purposes are made to meet specific objectives and not primarily because of their fiscal policy effects. Other important objectives must be merged with the goals of full employment, price stability, and economic growth. Therefore, government programs may have contradictory effects upon employment and inflation. Understanding these effects is complicated also by the time lags that occur before action taken pursuant to a specific policy begins to affect overall levels of employment, output, and prices.

In spite of these difficulties, policymakers and the general public continue to examine and debate the overall stabilization effects of public policy actions, because the consequences are so important. Citizens should understand the role of conflicting objectives and the limitations on the effectiveness of economic stabilization policies in order to develop realistic expectations about what can be accomplished with taxation, spending, and monetary policies.

BENCHMARKS

*At the completion of **Grade 12**, students will know that:*

1. Fiscal policies are decisions to change spending and tax levels by the federal government. These decisions are adopted to influence national levels of output, employment, and prices.

2. In the short run, increasing federal spending and/or reducing taxes can promote more employment and output, but these policies also put upward pressure on the price level and interest rates. Decreased federal spending and/or increased taxes tend to lower price levels and interest rates, but they reduce employment and output levels in the short run.

3. In the long run, the interest-rate effects of fiscal policies lead to changes in private investment spending by businesses and individuals that partially, if not entirely, offset the output and employment effects of fiscal policy.

4. The federal government's annual budget is balanced when its revenues from taxes and user fees equal its expenditures. The government runs a budget deficit when its expenditures exceed its revenues. The government runs a surplus when its revenues exceed its expenditures.

5. When the government runs a budget deficit, it must borrow from individuals, corporations, or financial institutions to finance that deficit.

6. The national debt is the total amount of money the federal government owes. This is the accumulated net sum of its annual deficits and surpluses. The government pays interest on the money it borrows to finance the national debt.

7. In the long run, inflation results from increases in a nation's money supply that exceed increases in its output of goods and services.

8. Monetary policies are decisions by the Federal Reserve System that lead to changes in the supply of money and the availability of credit. Changes in the money supply can influence overall levels of spending, employment, and prices in the economy by inducing changes in interest rates charged for credit and by affecting the levels of personal and business investment spending.

9. The major monetary policy tool that the Federal Reserve System uses is open market purchases or sales of government securities. Other policy tools used by the Federal Reserve System include increasing or decreasing the discount rate charged on loans it makes to commercial banks and raising or lowering reserve requirements for commercial banks.

*At the completion of **Grade 12**, students will use this knowledge to:*

1. Identify historical examples of fiscal policies and explain whether these policies were adopted to influence levels of output, employment, prices, or all three.

2. Outline the fiscal policies they would recommend to correct each of the following: (1) rising unemployment, and (2) rising inflation. Explain each recommendation.

3. Explain why an additional $2 billion of federal spending on highways, financed by federal government borrowing, can reduce private investment spending in the economy in the long run.

4. Determine whether the budget is in surplus, in deficit, or balanced, and whether the effect upon the economy is contractionary, expansionary, or neutral if the government receives $800 billion in taxes and (1) government spending is $800 billion; (2) government spending is $900 billion; (3) government spending is $700 billion.

5. Explain that the federal debt is financed through the sale of government securities and identify the percentage of debt owed to foreigners.

6. Explain the difference between the budget deficit and the national debt. Then determine how long it would take to pay off all of the national debt at the current rate of GDP if all GDP were devoted to that purpose.

7. Explain why inflation occurs after participating in two rounds of an auction

where the number of goods available remains constant, but the money in circulation increases in round two.

8. Write an article for the business section of the local newspaper explaining what monetary policy is and how changes in monetary policy affect the money supply and interest rates. Using this information, advise a teenager about taking out a car loan and his/her opportunities for obtaining summer employment in the construction trade when the Federal Reserve is contracting the money supply.

9. Play the roles of members of the Federal Open Market Committee and decide for each of the headlines below whether they would recommend an expansionary policy or a contractionary policy and whether government securities should be purchased or sold.

Newspaper headlines: *Unemployment Rate Soars*
New Housing Starts Rise
CPI Rises for Third Consecutive Month

OVERVIEW/EconomicsAmerica Materials

Grades K-4

An exemplary economic education curriculum for the early grades draws on the unique experiences that students bring to the classroom. Students have economic knowledge gained from their family, school, and community experiences. They also have a broader perspective of the world gained indirectly from television, movies, and travel. The National Council on Economic Education's **Economics**America curriculums build on this knowledge, addressing the economic concepts with increasing sophistication as students move from kindergarten to fourth grade.

EconomicsAmerica curriculums also have a strong interdisciplinary emphasis. The lessons for grades K-4 present economic content and offer a variety of suggestions for reinforcing this content in other subject areas, such as mathematics, science, language arts, and social studies. In addition, many lessons offer ideas for enriching economics by including activities that involve the community and the family.

Most of the K-4 curriculums include a series of lessons that can be taught as independent lessons or as a unit. Each curriculum offers ways to integrate economics into other subject areas. These instructional packages include the *Master Curriculum Guides: Teaching Strategies K-2* and *Teaching Strategies 3-4, Personal Finance Economics: Pocketwise* for grades K-2 and *$mart $pending and $aving* for grades 3-5, and the video series *Econ and Me* for grades 2-4.

Other curriculum packages are designed to be taught as a unit and the lessons are presented sequentially. *Choices & Changes: Work, Human Resources, and Choices* focuses on the link between education and productivity. Students learn about what skills, knowledge, and capital resources workers need to do their work. *Kindereconomy+* is a multidisciplinary learning society for primary grades. It provides a comprehensive instructional sequence with activities that motivate students by presenting concepts in a meaningful way, one that is applicable to their own lives and experiences. *The Community Publishing Company* teaches economic concepts through a study of the community and through the production and sale of a book that the students write about their community.

Capsule Summaries of EconomicsAmerica Publications: Grades K-4

Choices & Changes: Work, Human Resources, and Choice

Primary level students discover what being a worker means by interviewing workers from the community. These interviews teach them about goods and services and what skills, knowledge, and capital resources workers need to do the work. By applying what they have learned in activities such as making learning puzzles and teaching what they have learned to other students, students begin to set goals, make a plan to reach their goals and follow through on the plan.

The Community Publishing Company

After studying their communities, students write reports about their experiences, form a publishing company, and manufacture and sell a book of their writings.

Econ and Me

This program consists of five 15-minute video lessons. Each lesson focuses on a specific concept: scarcity, opportunity cost, consumption, production, and interdependence. The instructional manual offers suggestions for extending and reinforcing the economic concepts through mathematics and language arts.

Kindereconomy+

Kindereconomy+, a set of real-world experiences, emphasizes the decision-making concepts of economics. The program integrates economics with mathematics, language arts, and performing arts. This is a one-semester curriculum that introduces basic economic concepts to students in the primary grades.

Master Curriculum Guide: Teaching Strategies K-2

This publication has 25 lessons grouped around five clusters of economic concepts. These are economic wants and consumers; resources and producers; scarcity, choice and opportunity cost; specialization and interdependence; and money, markets, and exchange. Each cluster contains three active, engaging lessons that introduce the new concepts, followed by a learning center activity and a bulletin board activity. Suggestions are included for incorporating the concepts into mathematics, science, music, and language arts and for making connections with the family and the community.

Master Curriculum Guides: Teaching Strategies 3-4
This publication includes 15 lessons on a number of economic concepts including resources, opportunity cost, productivity, competition, circular flow, barter, money, taxes, supply, demand, and an entrepreneurship simulation. A variety of suggestions are offered to reinforce the economic content in other subjects. The lessons also include Family Corner, ideas for involving family members in the classroom; Community Corner, ideas for bringing the community into the classroom; and Children's Literature, an annotated list of related trade books.

Personal Finance Economics: Pocketwise
Pocketwise consists of fourteen lessons that focus on four personal finance concepts—money management, spending, saving, and credit. The lessons can be taught as a unit or as independent lessons. All lessons begin with a story that the teacher reads to the students. The story is followed with discussion questions and activities which require individual student work, whole class exercises and cooperative learning groups. A CONNECT section in each lesson provides optional activities that integrate personal finance with other subject areas and includes a list of supplementary selections from children's literature that reinforce all or part of a lesson.

Personal Finance Economics:
$mart $pending and $aving
This publication includes 10 lessons that help students develop the skills to make better spending, saving and borrowing decisions. These lessons teach them the importance of money management skills which are a critical part of life-long consumer success. Each lesson includes a CONNECT suggestion that provides ideas for incorporating the lesson's concepts into other subject areas. CONNECT also includes activities and a bibliography of resources for parents to use to help their children learn about the money management skills presented in the lesson.

GRADES 5-8

In the intermediate and middle school grades, an economics curriculum builds on knowledge gained in earlier grades and addresses economic concepts with increasing sophistication. The instructional activities at each grade level reflect the developmental characteristics of students at each grade level.

In fifth and sixth grades students can entertain more than one idea, take on the perspective of others, and tackle complex problems. This age group identifies themselves as members of a group. Yet, these students begin to think of themselves as individuals and think about their roles in the world. They want to make decisions for themselves and begin to express a desire for independence.

By seventh and eighth grades, students can examine their individual societal roles both now and in the future. They also focus on how groups of people participate in society as consumers, life-long decision makers, workers, savers, citizens, and global participants.

In grades 5-8, economics is integrated across the curriculum into mathematics, language arts, science, and social studies. The National Council on Economic Education's **Economics**America materials have a strong interdisciplinary emphasis providing lessons that can be infused into a variety of content areas. These lessons offer suggestions on how to reinforce critical thinking, creative thinking and cooperative learning.

Each lesson in *Master Curriculum Guide: Teaching Strategies 5-6* offers suggestions for reinforcing the economic concepts within other subject areas such as mathematics and language arts. These lessons also offer ideas for bringing the community into the classroom and for using the newspaper as a resource. The growing ability of students in grades 5-6 to combine ideas enables them to use the models, flow charts, and graphs that are used extensively in the lessons.

To prepare students to be more effective participants and citizens in a global society, *Focus: Middle School Economics* includes six units focusing on roles common to members of society. Each unit presents economic content relevant to a role students have or will have in the future as consumers, workers, savers, citizens, decision makers and global participants. All the lessons offer suggestions on ways to connect the content with other curricular content areas such as mathematics, language arts, and reading.

Teachers in middle school where social studies is departmentalized will find *United States History: Eyes on the Economy* and *Taxes in U.S. History* helpful for infusing economics into U.S. history. *Geography: Focus on Economics* provides lessons showing connections and interrelationships between economics and geography.

Other NCEE publications appropriate for grades 5-8 include *The International News Journal; Economics and the Environment: EcoDetectives;* and *Choices* &

Changes: You Can Be an Inventor (EII), Choices, the Economy, and You (JI), and *Choice Making, Productivity, and Planning (JIII).*

Capsule Summaries of EconomicsAmerica Publications: Grades 5-8

Choices & Changes

Choices & Changes demonstrates the critical link between education and future productivity in society through innovative lessons and fun-filled activities that teach key economic understandings. This program has three units appropriate for the middle grades. These are *You Can Be an Inventor (EII), Choices, the Economy and You (JI),* and *Choice Making, Productivity, and Planning (JIII).*

In *You Can Be an Inventor (EII),* intermediate level students learn about successful inventions and inventors. The students create inventions from scrounged materials, conduct market surveys for their products, and finally open a market for their inventions.

Students in grades 6-8 learn the costs and benefits of various alternatives in a classroom version of "Let's Make a Deal" in *Choices, the Economy, and You.* Lesson activities help students see the short- and long-term consequences of their actions, how their actions affect others, and what is needed to be a productive member in the workforce.

In *Choice Making, Productivity, and Planning* (JIII) for grades 8-9 students look toward the future. They conduct informational interviews, practice completing job applications, and learn what employers are looking for in their employees.

Economics and the Environment: EcoDetectives

This series of 18 lessons helps students address environmental issues. The lessons introduce economic reasoning and show students how to apply it to environmental problems in engaging ways. The title, *EcoDetectives,* indicates the role students play in the program—they become detectives as they solve persistent environmental mysteries.

Focus: Middle School Economics

This volume focuses on the six societal roles emphasized in **Economics**America: lifelong decision maker, knowledgeable consumer, productive worker, responsible citizen, prudent saver and global participant.

Geography: Focus on Economics

Students examine the connections and interrelationships between geography and economics, focusing on two specific geographical perspectives: the spatial perspective and the ecological perspective.

The International News Journal, Inc.

This program teaches economic concepts through regular classroom subjects including reading, language arts, geography, and mathematics. Students in the intermediate grades become aware of the world around them as they study trade relationships between the United States and seven other countries. They research and write articles for a news journal, form a classroom corporation, and then market and sell their product to the community.

Master Curriculum Guide: Teaching Strategies 5-6

This publication includes 15 lessons on the three basic economic questions, demand, production, supply, market clearing price, and government policy and regulations. Each lesson includes activities that reinforce critical and creative thinking and cooperative learning. Lessons also include suggestions for family activities, community involvement, and newspaper and language arts activities.

Personal Finance Economics: Money in the Middle

Money in the Middle responds to the questions: how can students use economic knowledge to make better decisions in real-world situations in which they participate as spenders, savers, borrowers, and managers of money? *Money in the Middle* has two to three lessons on each topic.

Taxes in U.S. History

Three 20-minute video programs develop students' understanding of the economics of taxation. Students learn how tax policies of the past have contributed to the policies of today.

United States History: Eyes on the Economy

This program focuses sharply on reasoning by presenting issues and events from the past as mysteries. Students see historical events more clearly and understand economics more deeply as they solve the mysteries.

Grades 9-12

An exemplary secondary economics curriculum integrates economics into social studies, history, consumer education, and business education classes. The economic education curriculum should be capped off with a semester or yearlong required course. Higher-ability students should be encouraged to complete Advanced Placement courses in microeconomics and macroeconomics.

The National Council on Economic Education offers **Economics**America publications that provide numerous lessons that can be integrated into history and social studies courses in the high school curriculum. A good way to begin infusing economics into history is to use the *Focus* books on world history and U.S. history. Teachers who want to go further should consider the two-volume set *United States History: Eyes on the Economy*. This publication helps students analyze economic history by presenting issues and events from the past as mysteries to be solved.

Civics and government teachers should review *Civics and Government: Focus on Economics*. Geography teachers will find lessons showing connections and interrelationships between geography and economics in *Geography: Focus on Economics*. Environmental economics is covered in *Economics and the Environment*, which explores the complementary relationship between the natural resources of the environment and an individual's economic well-being.

Consumer and business education teachers will find two publications particularly useful. *Personal Decision Making: Focus on Economics* applies economic concepts to budgeting, career planning, credit management, consumer purchasing, and housing. *Personal Finance Economics: Wallet Wisdom* provides activities requiring students to use economic knowledge to make better decisions as savers, spenders, borrowers, and managers of money. *Economics and Entrepreneurship, Teaching Strategies* challenges students to solve problems as they establish entrepreneurial enterprises.

A high school that is serious about economic literacy needs a separate economics course at least one semester in length. The starting point for such a course is *Focus: High School Economics*. The 20 lessons in this publication stress active, group-oriented, hands-on (and sometimes foot-moving) activities for high school students.

A second outstanding resource is *Capstone: The Nation's High School Economics Course*, which contains over 50 lessons that teach critical thinking and economic reasoning skills.

Economics at Work is a multimedia, contextual curriculum combining videodisc, print, and computer software into a comprehensive, one-semester course. Almost all the standards are taught in this curriculum package.

Other NCEE publications contain lessons that would be useful for the high school economics course. International economics is featured in *Economies in Transition: Command to Market* and *International Trade, Teaching Strategies*. Lessons from *Learning from the Market: Integrating The Stock Market Game™ across the Curriculum* can be taught in any course that uses *The Stock Market Game™*.

Finally, *Advanced Placement Economics* consists of two student workbooks and a Teacher Resource Manual for teaching the complete college-level economics course to high school students. It covers all the standards and much more. This program is keyed to the College Board's recommended course syllabus and prepares students for the Advanced Placement tests in microeconomics and macroeconomics.

Capsule Summaries of EconomicsAmerica Publications: Grades 9-12

Advanced Placement Economics
This is the only instructional package available for teaching complete college-level economics to high school students. This newly revised program is keyed to the College Board's recommended course syllabus, meets every syllabus requirement, and prepares students for all Advanced Placement economics tests.

Capstone: The Nation's High School Economics Course
Students use economic analysis to solve mysteries with 58 lively, easy-to-teach lessons in critical thinking and economic reasoning for either one- or two-class sessions. Lesson plans are in the Teacher Resource Manual.

Civics and Government: Focus on Economics
Students learn that economic decision making is part of political choice and that ignorance of economics in today's world prevents citizens from being able to make informed choices in their lives.

Economics and Entrepreneurship, Teaching Strategies
This publication challanges students to solve problems as they establish entrepreneurial enterprises. Students analyze and solve problems by applying economic concepts to entrepreneurial problems.

Economics and the Environment
This publication helps students understand the crucial relationship between economic activity and environmental protection. Using economics, students discover how and when the natural resources of the environment can be used.

Economics at Work
Economics at Work is a multimedia, contextual economic curriculum combining videodisc, print, and computer software into a comprehensive, one-semester course designed around five major economic activities. Each activity is organized into one of five instructional modules: producing, exchanging, consuming, saving, and investing.

Economies in Transition: Command to Market
These 10 lessons help U.S. students understand the challenges facing the former Soviet Union, the Baltic States, and the Central European countries during the transition to new and different economic systems.

Focus: High School Economics
A revision and update of the highly successful high school *Master Curriculum Guide,* this publication has new lessons on topics such as the stock market, public choice, and aggregate supply and demand.

Geography: Focus on Economics
Students examine the connections and interrelationships between geography and economics, focusing on two specific geographical perspectives: the spatial perspective and the ecological perspective.

International Trade, Teaching Strategies
This volume presents 23 complete lessons that enable students to apply economic concepts and principles to the global marketplace.

Learning from the Market: Integrating the Stock Market Game™ across the Curriculum
This resource manual helps teachers connect *The Stock Market Game™* to the principles of economics within the context of the existing curriculum. Lesson plans and activities involve students in economics, other social studies, language arts, and personal finance.

Personal Decision Making: Focus on Economics
Students see connections between their classroom learning and their real-world experiences in budgeting, career planning, credit management, and housing.

Personal Finance Economics: Wallet Wisdom
Wallet Wisdom responds to the question: how can students use economic knowledge to make better decisions in real-world situations in which they participate as spenders, savers, borrowers, and managers of money? *Wallet Wisdom* has two or three lessons on each topic, revealing the power of economic analysis in decision-making situations.

United States History: Eyes on the Economy
This program focuses sharply on reasoning by presenting issues and events from the past as mysteries. Students see historical events more clearly and understand economics more deeply as they solve the mysteries.

United States History: Focus on Economics
Historical events and current events are raw material for analysis of social history. Students recognize connections and patterns as they develop an understanding of the human experience.

World History: Focus on Economics
Students discover that from an economic standpoint, the history of the world is the history of people and nations making decisions about how to use their scarce resources.

EconomicsAmerica Materials
Grades K-4

Content Standard 1, Benchmark 1

Choices & Changes: Work, Human Resources, and Choices
Part 2, Days 6 & 7......I Make Choices and I Have Alternatives

Choices & Changes: You Can Be an Inventor: Human Capital and Entrepreneurship
Part 1, Day 3 ....I Can Create Something Valuable

Econ and Me
Lesson 1......................Scarcity

MCG, K-2
Lesson 1......................Wants From A to Z
Lesson 4......................Learning Center: Winning Wants
Lesson 11....................Alligator Annie and the Scarcity Adventure
Lesson 12....................Opportunities for Appreciation
Lesson 14....................Learning Center: Choice Train
Lesson 15....................Scarcity Bulletin Board: Balloon Trip

MCG, 3-4
Lesson 1......................Everybody Wants Everything
Lesson 4......................Olympic-Minded Decisions
Lesson 9......................A Cracker Jack Lesson

Personal Finance Economics K-2: Pocketwise
Lesson 4......................Consumers Choose to Spend
Lesson 9......................Budgeting Is a Way to Plan for Saving

Personal Finance Economics 3-5: $mart $pending and $aving
Lesson 1......................Decisions! Decisions! Decisions!
Lesson 2......................To Choose Is to Refuse
Lesson 7......................Why? How? Where?

Content Standard 1, Benchmark 2

Choices & Changes: You Can Be an Inventor: Human Capital and Entrepreneurship
Part 1, Day 1 ....I Can Be an Inventor
Part 1, Day 2 ....People Want New Things
Part 1, Day 3 ....I Can Create Something Valuable

The Community Publishing Company
Lesson 3......................Communities Change
Lesson 4......................Communities Today
Lesson 6......................Our Community
Lesson 7......................Community Interdependence
Lesson 8......................Mini-Mall

Econ and Me
Lesson 3......................Consumption

MCG, K-2
Lesson 1......................Wants From A to Z
Lesson 2......................Consumer Reflections
Lesson 3......................Foods Around the World
Lesson 4......................Learning Center: Winning Wants

MCG, 3-4
Lesson 1......................Everybody Wants Everything

Personal Finance Economics K-2: Pocketwise
Lesson 4......................Consumer Choose to Spend
Lesson 9......................Budgeting Is a Way to Plan for Saving

Personal Finance Economics 3-5: $mart $pending and $aving
Lesson 1......................Decisions! Decisions! Decisions!
Lesson 2......................To Choose Is to Refuse

Content Standard 1, Benchmark 3

Choices & Changes: Work, Human Resources, and Choices
Part 1, Day 2 ....Workers Make Goods and Provide Services
Part 1, Day 7 ....Workers on Their Jobs

Choices & Changes: You Can Be an Inventor: Human Capital and Entrepreneurship
Part 1, Day 1 ....I Can Be an Inventor
Part 1, Day 2 ....People Want New Things

The Community Publishing Company
Lesson 2......................Community Resources
Lesson 5......................My Community
Lesson 6......................Our Community

Econ and Me
Lesson 3......................Consumption

MCG, K-2
Lesson 2......................Consumer Reflections
Lesson 3......................Foods Around the World
Lesson 4......................Learning Center: Winning Wants

MCG, 3-4
Lesson 2......................Service With a Smile

Personal Finance Economics K-2: Pocketwise
Lesson 3......................Money Lets Me Choose
Lesson 4......................Consumer Choose to Spend

Personal Finance Economics 3-5: $mart $pending and $aving
Lesson 1......................Decisions! Decisions! Decisions!
Lesson 2......................To Choose Is to Refuse

Content Standard 1, Benchmark 4

Choices & Changes: Work, Human Resources, and Choices
Part 1, Day 2 ....Workers Make Goods and Provide Services
Part 1, Day 7 ....Workers on their Jobs

Choices & Changes: You Can Be an Inventor: Human Capital and Entrepreneurship
Part 1, Day 1 ....I Can Be an Inventor
Part 1, Day 2 ....People Want New Things

The Community Publishing Company
Lesson 2......................Community Resources
Lesson 5......................My Community
Lesson 6......................Our Community

Econ and Me
Lesson 3......................Consumption

MCG, K-2
Lesson 2......................Consumer Reflections
Lesson 3......................Foods Around the World
Lesson 4......................Learning Center: Winning Wants
Lesson 5......................People Movers Bulletin Board

MCG, 3-4
Lesson 2......................Service With a Smile

Personal Finance Economics K-2: Pocketwise
Lesson 3......................Money Lets Me Choose
Lesson 4......................Consumers Choose to Spend

Personal Finance Economics 3-5: $mart $pending and $aving
Lesson 1......................Decisions! Decisions! Decisions!
Lesson 2......................To Choose Is to Refuse

Content Standard 1, Benchmark 5

Choices & Changes: Work, Human Resources, and Choices
Part 1, Day 7 ....Workers on their Jobs

Choices & Changes: You Can Be an Inventor: Human Capital and Entrepreneurship
Part 1, Day 1 ....I Can Be an Inventor
Part 1, Day 2 ....People Want New Things
Part 1, Day 3 ....I Can Create Something Valuable

The Community Publishing Company
Lesson 2......................Community Resources
Lesson 3......................Communities Change
Lesson 4......................Communities Today
Lesson 21....................Resources for the Publishing Company

Econ and Me
Lesson 1......................Scarcity

Content Standard 1, Benchmark 6

Content Standard 1, Benchmark 7

Content Standard 1, Benchmark 8

The Community Publishing Company
    Lesson 5......................My Community
    Lesson 6......................Our Community

Econ and Me
    Lesson 3......................Consumption

MCG, K-2
    Lesson 2......................Consumer Reflections
    Lesson 5......................People Movers Bulletin Board

Personal Finance Economics K-2: Pocketwise
    Lesson 4......................Consumers Choose to Spend

Personal Finance Economics 3-5: $mart $pending and $aving
    Lesson 1......................Decisions! Decisions! Decisions!

Content Standard 1, Benchmark 9

Choices & Changes: Work, Human Resources, and Choices
    Part 1, Days 5 & 6......Worker Use Human Resources
    Part 2, Days 1 & 2......I Can Use My Human Resources to Make a Good

Choices & Changes: You Can Be an Inventor: Human Capital and Entrepreneurship
    Part 1, Day 1 ....I Can Be an Inventor
    Part 3, Day 2 ....We Have Skills and Knowledge

The Community Publishing Company
    Lesson 2......................Community Resources
    Lesson 3......................Communities Change
    Lesson 4......................Communities Today
    Lesson 21....................Resources for the Publishing Company

Econ and Me
    Lesson 4......................Production

MCG, K-2
    Lesson 6......................Mystery Workers
    Lesson 9......................Learning Center: Producer Pigs
    Lesson 10....................Bulletin Board: Art Gallery

MCG, 3-4
    Lesson 2......................Service With a Smile
    Lesson 9......................A Cracker Jack Lesson

Content Standard 1, Benchmark 10

The Community Publishing Company
    Lesson 2......................Community Resources
    Lesson 3......................Communities Change
    Lesson 4......................Communities Today

Econ and Me
    Lesson 4......................Production

MCG, K-2

MCG, 3-4

Content Standard 1, Benchmark 11

Choices & Changes: Work, Human Resources, and Choices

Choices & Changes: You Can Be an Inventor: Human Capital and Entrepreneurship

The Community Publishing Company

Econ and Me

MCG, K-2

MCG, 3-4

Personal Finance Economics K-2: Pocketwise

Content Standard 1, Benchmark 12

Choices & Changes: Work, Human Resources, and Choices

Choices & Changes: You Can Be an Inventor: Human Capital and Entrepreneurship

Content Standard 1, Benchmark 13

Content Standard 1, Benchmark 14

Content Standard 1, Benchmark 15

Content Standard 2, Benchmark 1

Content Standard 2, Benchmark 2

Content Standard 2, Benchmark 3

Content Standard 3, Benchmark 1

Content Standard 3, Benchmark 2

Content Standard 4, Benchmark 1

Content Standard 4, Benchmark 2

Choices & Changes: Work, Human Resources, and Choices
Part 3, Days 1 & 2......I Can Set and Reach My Goals
Part 3, Days 3 & 4......I Can Overcome Obstacles in Reaching My Goals

Personal Finance Economics K-2: Pocketwise
Lesson 7......................Advertising Influences Spending Decisions

Personal Finance Economics 3-5: $mart $pending and $aving
Lesson 4......................Why Do I Want All This Stuff?
Lesson 7......................Why? How? Where?

Content Standard 4, Benchmark 3

Choices & Changes: Work, Human Resources, and Choices
Part 3, Days 1 & 2......I Can Set and Reach My Goals
Part 3, Days 3 & 4......I Can Overcome Obstacles in Reaching My Goals

The Community Publishing Company
Lesson 30....................Advertising

MCG, 3-4
Lesson 12....................A Classy Competition
Lesson 15....................An Entrepreneurial Experience Extraordinaire

Personal Finance Economics K-2: Pocketwise
Lesson 7......................Advertising Influences Spending Decisions

Personal Finance Economics 3-5: $mart $pending and $aving
Lesson 4......................Why Do I Want All This Stuff?
Lesson 7......................Why? How? Where?

Content Standard 4, Benchmark 4

The Community Publishing Company
Lesson 8......................Mini-Mall

MCG, 3-4
Lesson 12....................A Classy Competition
Lesson 15....................An Entrepreneurial Experience Extraordinaire

Personal Finance Economics K-2: Pocketwise
Lesson 7......................Advertising Influences Spending Decisions

Personal Finance Economics 3-5: $mart $pending and $aving
Lesson 4......................Why Do I Want All This Stuff?
Lesson 7......................Why? How? Where?

Content Standard 5, Benchmark 1

MCG, K-2
Lesson 21....................His Barter Is Worse Than His Bite
Lesson 22....................Birthday Bear

MCG, 3-4
Lesson 7......................Let's Trade

Content Standard 5, Benchmark 2

MCG, K-2
Lesson 21....................His Barter Is Worse Than His Bite
Lesson 22....................Birthday Bear

MCG, 3-4
Lesson 7......................Let's Trade

Content Standard 5, Benchmark 3

Choices & Changes: You Can Be an Inventor: Human Capital and Entrepreneurship
Part 1, Day 2 ....People Want New Things

The Community Publishing Company
Lesson 8......................Mini-Mall

MCG, K-2
Lesson 21....................His Barter Is Worse Than His Bite
Lesson 22....................Birthday Bear

MCG, 3-4
Lesson 7......................Let's Trade

Content Standard 6, Benchmark 1

Choices & Changes: You Can Be an Inventor: Human Capital and Entrepreneurship
Part 2, Day 6 ....The Proof in the Pudding

The Community Publishing Company
Lesson 7......................Community Interdependence
Lesson 9......................Visiting a Business
Lesson 11....................The Badge Factory
Lesson 28....................Preparation for Production

Econ and Me
Lesson 5......................Interdependence

MCG, K-2
Lesson 16....................An Interdependent Bunch
Lesson 17....................Spotlight on Specialists
Lesson 18....................The Baker Wants a Pair of Shoes
Lesson 19....................Learning Center: School Connections
Lesson 20....................Bulletin Board: Showcasing Specialists

MCG, 3-4
Lesson 5......................Getting More Out of Less
Lesson 15....................An Entrepreneurial Experience Extraordinaire

Content Standard 6, Benchmark 2

The Community Publishing Company
Lesson 9......................Visiting a Business
Lesson 11....................The Badge Factory
Lesson 27....................Job Application

MCG, K-2
  Lesson 25.....................Teddy Bear Picnic

MCG, 3-4
  Lesson 9.......................A Cracker Jack Lesson
  Lesson 14.....................Orange Juice Jubilee

Personal Finance Economics K-2: Pocketwise
  Lesson 5.......................Spending Decisions Go On and On

Content Standard 7, Benchmark 2

The Community Publishing Company
  Lesson 5.......................My Community
  Lesson 8.......................Mini-Mall
  Lesson 10.....................The Pencil Choice
  Lesson 13.....................Results of the Community Interview
  Lesson 22.....................Production Questions
  Lesson 23.....................Production and Pricing Decisions

MCG, K-2
  Lesson 23.....................To Market, To Market
  Lesson 25.....................Bulletin Board: Teddy Bear Picnic

MCG, 3-4
  Lesson 6.......................Circles Within Circles

Content Standard 7, Benchmark 3

Choices & Changes: You Can Be an Inventor: Human Capital and Entrepreneurship
  Part 1, Day 2 ....People Want New Things

The Community Publishing Company
  Lesson 1.......................A Community Success Story
  Lesson 7.......................Community Interdependence
  Lesson 8.......................Mini-Mall

Econ and Me
  Lesson 3.......................Consumption
  Lesson 4.......................Production

MCG, K-2
  Lesson 2.......................Consumer Reflections
  Lesson 8.......................Producer Charades
  Lesson 23.....................To Market, To Market

MCG, 3-4
  Lesson 6.......................Circles Within Circles

Content Standard 8, Benchmark 1

Choices & Changes: You Can Be an Inventor: Human Capital and Entrepreneurship
  Part 2, Day 1 ....Will a Good Idea Sell?
  Part 2, Day 2 ....The Basics: What? How Many? and How to Produce?
  Part 3, Day 1 ....Surplus or Shortage?

The Community Publishing Company
Lesson 10....................The Pencil Choice

MCG, 3-4
Lesson 9......................A Cracker Jack Lesson
Lesson 11....................Those Golden Jeans

Content Standard 9, Benchmark 1

MCG, 3-4
Lesson 12....................A Classy Competition

Personal Finance Economics 3-5: $mart $pending and $aving
Lesson 4......................Why Do I Want All This Stuff?

Content Standard 9, Benchmark 2

MCG, 3-4
Lesson 12....................A Classy Competition

Personal Finance Economics K-2: Pocketwise
Lesson 7......................Advertising Influences Spending Decisions

Personal Finance Economics 3-5: $mart $pending and $aving
Lesson 4......................Why Do I Want All This Stuff?

Content Standard 10, Benchmark 1

The Community Publishing Company
Lesson 24....................Obtaining Resources on Credit
Lesson 25....................Obtaining a Bank Loan
Lesson 26....................Study Trip

MCG, 3-4
Lesson 14....................Orange Juice Jubilee

Personal Finance Economics K-2: Pocketwise
Lesson 8......................Why We Save
Lesson 9......................Budgeting Is a Way to Plan to Save

Personal Finance Economics 3-5: $mart $pending and $aving
Lesson 7......................Why? How? Where?

Content Standard 10, Benchmark 2

Econ and Me
Lesson 3......................Consumption

Personal Finance Economics K-2: Pocketwise
Lesson 8......................Why We Save
Lesson 9......................Budgeting Is a Way to Plan to Save
Lesson 10....................Saving Requires Waiting
Lesson 14....................Demonstrating Money Management

Personal Finance Economics 3-5: $mart $pending and $aving
Lesson 5......................The Grasshopper and the Ant

Content Standard 11, Benchmark 1

Content Standard 11, Benchmark 2

Content Standard 11, Benchmark 3

Content Standard 11, Benchmark 4

MCG, 3-4
    Lesson 2......................Service With a Smile

Content Standard 13, Benchmark 1

Choices & Changes: Work, Human Resources, and Choices
    Part 1, Day 1 ....The Work I Do
    Part 3, Day 5 ....I Can Learn From Other Workers
    Part 3, Day 6 ....Conducting Worker Interviews
    Part 3, Day 7 ....Seeing Myself as a Future Worker

Choices & Changes: You Can Be an Inventor: Human Capital and Entrepreneurship
    Part 1, Day 1 ....I Can Be an Inventor
    Part 2, Day 3 ....The Right Stuff

MCG, K-2
    Lesson 8......................Producer Charades

MCG, 3-4
    Lesson 2......................Service With a Smile
    Lesson 13....................The Working World

Personal Finance Economics K-2: Pocketwise
    Lesson 1......................A Very Good Day for Money

Content Standard 13, Benchmark 2

Choices & Changes: Work, Human Resources, and Choices
    Part 1, Day 1 ....The Work I Do

Choices & Changes: You Can Be an Inventor: Human Capital and Entrepreneurship
    Part 2, Days 4 & 5......Organizing Production
    Part 2, Day 6 ....The Proof in the Pudding

Econ and Me
    Lesson 3......................Consumption

MCG, 3-4
    Lesson 6......................Circles Within Circles
    Lesson 13....................The Working World

Personal Finance Economics K-2: Pocketwise
    Lesson 1......................A Very God Day for Money

Content Standard 14, Benchmark 1

Choices & Changes: You Can Be an Inventor: Human Capital and Entrepreneurship
    Part 1, Day 4 ....Traits for Success
    Part 3, Day 3 ....A Great Invention

The Community Publishing Company
    Lesson 22....................Production Questions

MCG, 3-4
    Lesson 14....................Orange Juice Jubilee

Content Standard 14, Benchmark 2

Choices & Changes: You Can Be an Inventor: Human Capital and Entrepreneurship
Part 1, Day 2 ....People Want New Things
Part 1, Day 3 ....I Can Create Something Valuable
Part 1, Day 4 ....Traits for Success
Part 2, Day 1 ....Will a Good Idea Sell?
Part 3, Day 3 ....A Great Invention

Content Standard 14, Benchmark 3

Choices & Changes: You Can Be an Inventor: Human Capital and Entrepreneurship
Part 1, Day 2 ....People Want New Things
Part 1, Day 4 ....Traits for Success
Part 2, Day 1 ....Will a Good Idea Sell?
Part 3, Day 3 ....A Great Invention

MCG, 3-4
Lesson 14....................Orange Juice Jubilee

Content Standard 15, Benchmark 1

Choices & Changes: Work, Human Resources, and Choices
Part 2, Days 1 & 2......I Can Use My Human Resources to Make a Good
Part 2, Day 3 ....I Can Improve My Human Resources With Practice
Part 2, Days 4 & 5......Teaching Others Builds Human Resources

Choices & Changes: You Can Be an Inventor: Human Capital and Entrepreneurship
Part 3, Day 2 ....We Have Skills and Knowledge

MCG, 3-4
Lesson 13....................The Working World

Content Standard 15, Benchmark 2

Choices & Changes: Work, Human Resources, and Choices
Part 2, Days 1 & 2......I Can Use My Human Resources to Make a Good
Part 2, Day 3 ....I Can Improve My Human Resources With Practice
Part 2, Days 4 & 5......Teaching Others Builds Human Resources

Choices & Changes: You Can Be an Inventor: Human Capital and Entrepreneurship
Part 3, Day 2 ....We Have Skills and Knowledge

MCG, 3-4
Lesson 13....................The Working World

Content Standard 15, Benchmark 3

Choices & Changes: Work, Human Resources, and Choices
Part 1, Days 3 & 4......Workers Use Capital Goods

Choices & Changes: You Can Be an Inventor: Human Capital and Entrepreneurship
Part 3, Day 2 ....We Have Skills and Knowledge

Content Standard 16, Benchmark 1

Econ and Me

Lesson 3......................Consumption

MCG, 3-4

Lesson 10....................A Taxing Situation

Content Standard 16, Benchmark 2

MCG, 3-4

Lesson 10....................A Taxing Situation

Content Standard 19, Benchmark 2

MCG, 3-4

Lesson 13....................The Working World

EconomicsAmerica Materials
Grades 5-8

Content Standard 1, Benchmark 4

Choices & Changes: Choices, the Economy, and You
Part 2, Days 5 & 6......Choices Make a Difference: Worker Interviews
Part 3, Day 2 ....Long- and Short-Term Consequences

Choices & Changes: Choice Making, Productivity, and Planning
Part 3, Day 2 ....Planning to Choose

Focus: Middle School Economics
Lesson 1......................The Path Not Taken
Lesson 14....................No Free Lunch

International News Journal
Lesson 5......................International Trade
Lesson 18....................Topics for the News Journal

MCG, 5-6
Lesson 1......................Choosing a House

Personal Finance Economics, 6-8: Money in the Middle
Lesson 1......................Check It Out
Lesson 8......................Who Gets the Money?
Lesson 9......................What Works for Us!

United States History, Eyes on the Economy, Vol. I
Unit 2, Lesson 1 ....The New World Was an Old World
Unit 3, Lesson 2 ....Be a Planet Planner
Unit 4, Lesson 2 ....The Costs and Benefits of Independence
Unit 5, Lesson 2 ....The Constitution: Ground Rules for the Economy
Unit 6, Lesson 1 ....The Tale of the Corset and the Necktie
Unit 6, Lesson 4 ....Cost Cutting is Fashionable
Unit 8, Lesson 1 ....Why Did the South Secede?
Unit 8, Lesson 2 ....The Economic Effects of the Civil War

Content Standard 1, Benchmark 5

Choices & Changes: Choices, the Economy, and You
Part 2, Day 3 ....Ways to Make Choices

Choices & Changes: Choice Making, Productivity, and Planning
Part 1, Day 2 ....Identifying and Choosing Among Alternatives
Part 1, Day 3 ....Choices: Benefits and Costs

Focus: Middle School Economics
Introductory Lesson..Economic Roll Call

International News Journal
Lesson 18....................Topics for the News Journal

Personal Finance Economics, 6-8: Money in the Middle
Lesson 1......................Check It Out
Lesson 2......................Party Planners
Lesson 3......................What Would You Do?

United States History, Eyes on the Economy, Vol. I
>> Unit 4, Lesson 1 ....Understanding the Colonial Economy
>> Unit 6, Lesson 1 ....The Tale of the Corset and the Necktie

Content Standard 2, Benchmark 1

Choices & Changes: Choice Making, Productivity, and Planning
>> Part 1, Day 2 ....Identifying and Choosing Among Alternatives
>> Part 1, Day 3 ....Choices: Benefits and Costs

Economics and the Environment: EcoDetectives
>> Lesson 5......................How Clean Is Clean Enough?

Focus: Middle School Economics
>> Lesson 2......................Give and Take

MCG, 5-6
>> Lesson 1......................Choosing a House

Personal Finance Economics, 6-8: Money in the Middle
>> Lesson 2......................Party Planners
>> Lesson 10....................At the Margin Education Pays!

United States History, Eyes on the Economy, Vol. I
>> Unit 4, Lesson 2 ....The Costs and Benefits of Independence
>> Unit 6, Lesson 5 ....Improving Transportation
>> Unit 7, Lesson 1 ....Saving and Investing in Razorback

Content Standard 3, Benchmark 1

MCG, 5-6
>> Lesson 1......................Choosing a House
>> Lesson 2......................What? How? For Whom?

Content Standard 3, Benchmark 2

United States History, Eyes on the Economy, Vol. I
>> Unit 5, Lesson 4 ....Entrepreneurship Case Study: Adam Smith

Content Standard 3, Benchmark 3

MCG, 5-6
>> Lesson 2......................What? How? For Whom?

Content Standard 3, Benchmark 4

United States History, Eyes on the Economy, Vol. I
>> Unit 5, Lesson 4 ....Entrepreneurship Case Study: Adam Smith

Content Standard 3, Benchmark 5

Focus: Middle School Economics
>> Lesson 7......................The T-riffic T's Company: Production Decisions

Content Standard 4, Benchmark 1

Content Standard 4, Benchmark 2

Unit 6, Lesson 5.........Improving Transportation
Unit 7, Lesson 1.........Saving and Investing in Razorback

Content Standard 4, Benchmark 3

United States History, Eyes on the Economy, Vol. I
Unit 1, Lesson 2.........The Hula Hoop Market of 1958
Unit 3, Lesson 2.........Be a Planet Planner
Unit 4, Lesson 1.........Understanding the Colonial Economy
Unit 4, Lesson 3.........Entrepreneurship Case Study: Eliza Lucas Pinckney
Unit 5, Lesson 2.........The Constitution: Ground Rules for the Economy
Unit 5, Lesson 4.........Entrepreneurship Case Study: Adam Smith
Unit 6, Lesson 5.........Improving Transportation
Unit 6, Lesson 7.........Entrepreneurship Case Study: Samuel Slater
Unit 7, Lesson 1.........Saving and Investing in Razorback

Content Standard 5, Benchmark 1

Focus: Middle School Economics
Lesson 3......................To Market, Which Market?

United States History, Eyes on the Economy, Vol. I
Unit 4, Lesson 1.........Understanding the Colonial Economy
Unit 4, Lesson 2.........The Costs and Benefits of Independence
Unit 4, Lesson 3.........Entrepreneurship Case Study: Eliza Lucas Pinckney
Unit 6, Lesson 1.........The Tale of the Corset and the Necktie

Content Standard 5, Benchmark 2

Focus: Middle School Economics
Lesson 16....................Frontier Specialists
Lesson 17....................Don't Fence Me Out

Geography: Focus on Economics
Lesson 6......................Limiting Trade

International News Journal
Lesson 5......................International Trade
Lesson 7......................Trade Among Businesses
Lesson 8......................Comparative Advantages

United States History, Eyes on the Economy, Vol. I
Unit 4, Lesson 1.........Understanding the Colonial Economy
Unit 4, Lesson 2.........The Costs and Benefits of Independence
Unit 4, Lesson 3.........Entrepreneurship Case Study: Eliza Lucas Pinckney
Unit 5, Lesson 1.........Problems Under the Articles of Confederation
Unit 5, Lesson 4.........Entrepreneurship Case Study: Adam Smith
Unit 6, Lesson 2.........Productivity Raises Output

Content Standard 5, Benchmark 3

Focus: Middle School Economics
Lesson 17.....................Don't Fence Me Out

United States History, Eyes on the Economy, Vol. I
Unit 6, Lesson 3 ....Lowell Workers and Producers Respond to Incentives

Content Standard 5, Benchmark 4

Focus: Middle School Economics
Lesson 13.....................An Island Economy
Lesson 17.....................Don't Fence Me Out

International News Journal
Lesson 4.....................Trading Partners Around the World
Lesson 9.....................What the United States Imports
Lesson 10.....................Japan and the United States are Trading Partners

United States History, Eyes on the Economy, Vol. I
Unit 4, Lesson 1 ....Understanding the Colonial Economy
Unit 4, Lesson 2 ....The Costs and Benefits of Independence

Content Standard 5, Benchmark 5

Focus: Middle School Economics
Lesson 13.....................An Island Economy

International News Journal
Lesson 4.....................Trading Partners Around the World
Lesson 9.....................What the United States Imports
Lesson 10.....................Japan and the United States are Trading Partners

United States History, Eyes on the Economy, Vol. I
Unit 4, Lesson 1 ....Understanding the Colonial Economy

Content Standard 5, Benchmark 6

Focus: Middle School Economics
Lesson 16.....................Frontier Specialists

International News Journal
Lesson 3.....................Similarities and Differences Around the World
Lesson 4.....................Trading Partnerships Around the World
Lesson 5.....................International Trade
Lesson 6.....................Individuals Benefit from Trade
Lesson 7.....................Trade Among Businesses
Lesson 8.....................Comparative Advantage
Lesson 9.....................What the United States Imports
Lesson 10.....................Japan and the United States are Trading Partners

United States History, Eyes on the Economy, Vol. I
Unit 1, Lesson 2 ....The United States' Past and the Global Economy
Unit 2, Lesson 2 ....Did Native Americans Act Economically?
Unit 4, Lesson 2 ....The Costs and Benefits of Independence

Unit 5, Lesson 4 ....Entrepreneurship Case Study: Adam Smith
Unit 6, Lesson 2 ....Productivity Raises Output

Content Standard 6, Benchmark 1

Choices & Changes: Choice Making, Productivity, and Planning
Part 2, Day 1 ....Changing Productivity
Part 2, Day 2 ....Human Capital and Productivity

Economics and the Environment: EcoDetectives
Lesson 13....................Will There Be Food for You?

International News Journal
Lesson 28....................Assembling the News Journal

MCG, 5-6
Lesson 7......................Widget Production

United States History, Eyes on the Economy, Vol. I
Unit 6, Lesson 2 ....Productivity Raises Output
Unit 6, Lesson 5 ....Improving Transportation

Content Standard 6, Benchmark 2

Focus: Middle School Economics
Lesson 16....................Frontier Specialists

International News Journal
Lesson 3......................Similarities and Differences Around the World
Lesson 5......................International Trade
Unit 8, Lesson 2 ....Economic Effects of the Civil War

United States History, Eyes on the Economy, Vol. I
Unit 5, Lesson 1 ....Problems Under the Articles of Confederation
Unit 5, Lesson 4 ....Entrepreneurship Case Study: Adam Smith
Unit 6, Lesson 2 ....Productivity Raises Output

Content Standard 6, Benchmark 3

Focus: Middle School Economics
Lesson 17....................Don't Fence Me Out!

United States History, Eyes on the Economy, Vol. I
Unit 5, Lesson 1 ....Problems Under the Articles of Confederation

Content Standard 7, Benchmark 1

MCG, 5-6
Lesson 11....................Market Balance
Lesson 12....................Market Madness

United States History, Eyes on the Economy, Vol. I
Unit 1, Lesson 3 ....The Hula Hoop Market of 1958

Content Standard 7, Benchmark 2

MCG, 5-6
Lesson 11....................Market Balance
Lesson 13....................Mind Your P's and Q's

United States History, Eyes on the Economy, Vol. I
Unit 1, Lesson 3.........The Hula Hoop Market of 1958

Content Standard 7, Benchmark 3

MCG, 5-6
Lesson 12....................Market Madness
Lesson 13....................Mind Your P's and Q's

United States History, Eyes on the Economy, Vol. I
Unit 1, Lesson 1.........Solving Economic Mysteries in U.S. History: A User's Guide
Unit 4, Lesson 3.........Entrepreneurship Case Study: Eliza Lucas Pinckney
Unit 5, Lesson 2.........The Constitution: Ground Rules for the Economy
Unit 5, Lesson 4.........Entrepreneurship Case Study: Adam Smith
Unit 6, Lesson 2.........Productivity Raises Output

Content Standard 7, Benchmark 4

Focus: Middle School Economics
Lesson 4....................How Much Will You Buy?

International News Journal
Lesson 31....................Selling the News Journal

MCG, 5-6
Lesson 12....................Market Madness
Lesson 13....................Mind Your P's and Q's

United States History, Eyes on the Economy, Vol. I
Unit 1, Lesson 3.........The Hula Hoop Market of 1958

Geography: Focus on Economics
Lesson 5....................Money Around the World

Content Standard 8, Benchmark 1

Focus: Middle School Economics
Lesson 4....................How Many Will You Buy?

MCG, 5-6
Lesson 4....................A Profusion of Confusion
Lesson 5....................Graphing Demand

United States History, Eyes on the Economy, Vol. I
Unit 1, Lesson 3.........The Hula Hoop Market of 1958

Content Standard 8, Benchmark 2

Focus: Middle School Economics
Lesson 8....................How Many Should We Sell?

MCG, 5-6

Content Standard 8, Benchmark 3

MCG, 5-6

Content Standard 8, Benchmark 4

Focus: Middle School Economics

MCG, 5-6

United States History, Eyes on the Economy, Vol. I

Content Standard 9, Benchmark 1

United States History, Eyes on the Economy, Vol. I

Content Standard 9, Benchmark 3

United States History, Eyes on the Economy, Vol. I

Content Standard 10, Benchmark 1

Focus: Middle School Economics

Personal Finance Economics, 6-8: Money in the Middle

United States History, Eyes on the Economy, Vol. I

Content Standard 11, Benchmark 1

Focus: Middle School Economics

Content Standard 11, Benchmark 3

United States History, Eyes on the Economy, Vol. I

Content Standard 13, Benchmark 1

Content Standard 13, Benchmark 2

Content Standard 13, Benchmark 3

Content Standard 13, Benchmark 4

Content Standard 13, Benchmark 5

Choices & Changes: Choices, the Economy, and You
> Part 1, Day 3 ....People Use Their Human Capital in the Economy
> Part 1, Day 4 ....I Am Part of the Economy

Choices & Changes: Choice Making, Productivity, and Planning
> Part 2, Day 2 ....Human Capital and Productivity
> Part 2, Day 3 ....Thinking About My Human Capital
> Part 2, Day 4 ....What Employers Want
> Part 2, Days 5 & 6......The Want Ads: What Do They Really Mean?
> Part 3, Day 2 ....Planning to Choose

United States History, Eyes on the Economy, Vol. I
> Unit 6, Lesson 3 ....Lowell Workers and Producers Respond to Incentives

Content Standard 14, Benchmark 1

Focus: Middle School Economics
> Lesson 1......................The Path Not Taken

United States History, Eyes on the Economy, Vol. I
> Unit 4, Lesson 3 ....Entrepreneurship Case Study: Eliza Lucas Pinckney
> Unit 5, Lesson 3 ....Entrepreneurship Case Study: George Mason

Content Standard 14, Benchmark 2

Focus: Middle School Economics
> Lesson 1......................The Path Not Taken
> Lesson 7......................The T-riffic T's Company: Production Decisions
> Lesson 9......................The Profit Puzzle

International News Journal
> Lesson 7......................Trade Among Businesses

United States History, Eyes on the Economy, Vol. I
> Unit 4, Lesson 3 ....Entrepreneurship Case Study: Eliza Lucas Pinckney
> Unit 6, Lesson 2 ....Productivity Raises Output
> Unit 6, Lesson 4 ....Cost Cutting is Fashionable
> Unit 6, Lesson 6 ....What is Investment?
> Unit 7, Lesson 1 ....Saving and Investing in Razorback

Content Standard 14, Benchmark 3

Focus: Middle School Economics
> Lesson 9......................The Profit Puzzle

MCG, 5-6
> Lesson 8......................Creative Toy Production

United States History, Eyes on the Economy, Vol. I
> Unit 6, Lesson 4 ....Cost Cutting Is Fashionable

Content Standard 14, Benchmark 4

Focus: Middle School Economics
Lesson 9......................The Profit Puzzle

MCG, 5-6
Lesson 8......................Creative Toy Production

Content Standard 14, Benchmark 5

Focus: Middle School Economics
Lesson 1......................The Path Not Taken

United States History, Eyes on the Economy, Vol. I
Unit 4, Lesson 3 ....Entrepreneurship Case Study: Eliza Lucas Pinckney
Unit 5, Lesson 3 ....Entrepreneurship Case Study: George Mason

Content Standard 15, Benchmark 1

Geography: Focus on Economics
Lesson 7......................Places and Productions
Lesson 8......................GDP and Life Expectancy

United States History, Eyes on the Economy, Vol. I
Unit 3, Lesson 1 ....Why Do Economies Grow?
Unit 6, Lesson 2 ....Productivity Raises Output
Unit 6, Lesson 5 ....Improving Transportation

Content Standard 15, Benchmark 2

Choices & Changes: Choice Making, Productivity, and Planning
Part 2, Day 1 ....Changing Productivity
Part 2, Day 2 ....Human Capital and Productivity

Economics and the Environment: EcoDetectives
Lesson 13....................Will There Be Food for You?

MCG, 5-6
Lesson 7......................Widget Production

United States History, Eyes on the Economy, Vol. I
Unit 6, Lesson 2 ....Productivity Raises Output

Content Standard 15, Benchmark 3

Choices & Changes: Choice Making, Productivity, and Planning
Part 3, Day 2 ....Planning to Choose

Focus: Middle School Economics
Lesson 7......................The T'riffic T's Company: Production Decisions

MCG, 5-6
Lesson 7......................Widget Production

United States History, Eyes on the Economy, Vol. I
Unit 3, Lesson 1 ....Why Do Economies Grow?
Unit 6, Lesson 2 ....Productivity Raises Output

Content Standard 15, Benchmark 4

Content Standard 16, Benchmark 1

Content Standard 16, Benchmark 2

Content Standard 16, Benchmark 4

Content Standard 16, Benchmark 5

Content Standard 18, Benchmark 1

Content Standard 18, Benchmark 2

Geography: Focus on Economics
Lesson 8......................GDP and Life Expectancy

Content Standard 18, Benchmark 3

MCG, 5-6
Lesson 3......................Dandy Dollars Takes a Trip

Content Standard 19, Benchmark 2

Choices & Changes: Choice Making, Productivity, and Planning
Part 2, Day 3 ....Thinking About My Human Capital

Content Standard 19, Benchmark 3

Focus: Middle School Economics
Lesson 6......................Inflation

United States History, Eyes on the Economy, Vol. I
Unit 7, Lesson 3.........Boom and Bust in the 1830s

Content Standard 19, Benchmark 4

Focus: Middle School Economics
Lesson 6......................Inflation

United States History, Eyes on the Economy, Vol. I
Unit 7, Lesson 3.........Boom and Bust in the 1830s

EconomicsAmerica Materials
Grades 9-12

Content Standard 1, Benchmark 1

Content Standard 2, Benchmark 1

Content Standard 2, Benchmark 2

Content Standard 2, Benchmark 3

Content Standard 2, Benchmark 4

Capstone

Civics and Government: Focus on Economics

Economics and the Environment

Focus: High School Economics

Geography: Focus on Economics

United States History: Focus on Economics

Content Standard 3, Benchmark 1

Capstone

Economics and the Environment

Economies in Transition: Command to Market

MCG–International Trade

United States History, Eyes on the Economy, Vol. II

World History: Focus on Economics

Content Standard 4, Benchmark 1

Capstone

Content Standard 4, Benchmark 2

Content Standard 5, Benchmark 1

Content Standard 5, Benchmark 2

Capstone

Civics and Government: Focus on Economics

Geography: Focus on Economics

MCG–International Trade

United States History, Eyes on the Economy, Vol. II

Content Standard 6, Benchmark 1

Capstone

Geography: Focus on Economics

MCG–International Trade

World History: Focus on Economics

Content Standard 6, Benchmark 2

Geography: Focus on Economics

Learning from the Market: Integrating the Stock Market Game™ across the Curriculum

United States History, Eyes on the Economy, Vol. II

World History: Focus on Economics
        Lesson 3......................Trade in Africa, 9th to 12th Centuries A.D

Content Standard 6, Benchmark 3

Capstone
        Unit 7, Lesson 3.........Why People Trade: Comparative Advantage

Geography: Focus on Economics
        Lesson 3......................Why Nations Trade

MCG–International Trade
        Lesson 3......................Why People and Nations Trade
        Lesson 4......................Trade and Specialization
        Lesson 9......................Trade Around the World

World History: Focus on Economics
        Lesson 3......................Trade in Africa, 9th to 12th Centuries A.D

Content Standard 6, Benchmark 4

Geography: Focus on Economics
        Lesson 3......................Why Nations Trade

MCG–International Trade
        Lesson 3......................Why People and Nations Trade
        Lesson 9......................Trade Around the World

Content Standard 7, Benchmark 1

Capstone
        Unit 2, Lesson 8.........When There Are Floors and Ceilings

Economics and the Environment
        Lesson 3......................What Are Spotted Owls, Timber Products, and Magical Stones
                                Really Worth?
        Lesson 6......................It's Fine as Long as It's Mine—All Mine!

Economies in Transition: Command to Market
        Lesson 1......................A Parking Lot Full of Incentives
        Lesson 6......................All for One, One for All—Well Maybe: Problems Within a Tightly
                                Controlled Industrial Structure

Focus: High School Economics
        Lesson 6......................Price Controls: Too Low or Too High

Learning from the Market: Integrating the Stock Market Game™ across the Curriculum
        Lesson 6......................How Are Stock Prices Determined?

MCG–Economics and Entrepreneurship
        Lesson 11....................What's the Right Price?

MCG–International Trade
        Lesson 10....................Trade Barriers
        Lesson 16....................Foreign Exchange and Foreign Currencies
        Lesson 17....................Rubles and the Dollars: The Tale of Two Currencies

United States History, Eyes on the Economy, Vol. II
   Unit 1, Lesson 3.........The Hula Hoop Market of 1958

Content Standard 7, Benchmark 2

Capstone
   Unit 2, Lesson 8.........When There Are Floors and Ceilings

Economies in Transition: Command to Market
   Lesson 1.....................A Parking Lot Full of Incentives
   Lesson 6.....................All for One, One for All—Well Maybe: Problems Within a
              Tightly Controlled Industrial Structure

Focus: High School Economics
   Lesson 6.....................Price Controls: Too Low or Too High

Learning from the Market: Integrating the Stock Market Game™ across the Curriculum
   Lesson 6.....................How Are Stock Prices Determined?

MCG–Economics and Entrepreneurship
   Lesson 11....................What's the Right Price?

MCG–International Trade
   Lesson 10....................Trade Barriers
   Lesson 17....................Rubles and the Dollars: The Tale of Two Currencies

United States History, Eyes on the Economy, Vol. II
   Unit 1, Lesson 3.........The Hula Hoop Market of 1958

Content Standard 7, Benchmark 3

Capstone
   Unit 2, Lesson 8.........When There Are Floors and Ceilings

Economics and the Environment
   Lesson 6.....................It's Fine as Long as It's Mine—All Mine!
   Lesson 17....................Crying "Wolf!" About Running Out of Natural Resources

Economies in Transition: Command to Market
   Lesson 1.....................A Parking Lot Full of Incentives
   Lesson 6.....................All for One, One for All—Well Maybe: Problems Within a
              Tightly Controlled Industrial Structure

Focus: High School Economics
   Lesson 6.....................Price Controls: Too Low or Too High

Learning from the Market: Integrating the Stock Market Game™ across the Curriculum
   Lesson 6.....................How Are Stock Prices Determined?

MCG–Economics and Entrepreneurship
   Lesson 11....................What's the Right Price?

MCG–International Trade
   Lesson 10....................Trade Barriers

Personal Decision Making: Focus on Economics
   Lesson 5.....................Price as a Rationing Method: How Does a Market Work?

United States History, Eyes on the Economy, Vol. II
    Unit 1, Lesson 3.........The Hula Hoop Market of 1958

Content Standard 7, Benchmark 4

Capstone
    Unit 7, Lesson 8.........Exchange Rates

Geography: Focus on Economics
    Lesson 5......................Money Around the World

MCG–International Trade
    Lesson 17....................Rubles and Dollars: The Tale of Two Currencies
    Lesson 18....................Exchange Rates

Personal Decision Making: Focus on Economics
    Lesson 15....................International Economics: Why Should You Care?

Content Standard 8, Benchmark 1

Capstone
    Unit 2, Lesson 7.........The Market Never Stands Still

Economics and the Environment
    Lesson 3......................What Are Spotted Owls, Timber Products, and Magical Stones
                            Really Worth?
    Lesson 15....................Halloween Treats and Nonrenewable Resources
    Lesson 18....................Recycling: A Tale of Two Markets

Focus: High School Economics
    Lesson 4......................The Market Never Stands Still
    Lesson 5......................Markets Interact

Learning from the Market: Integrating the Stock Market Game™ across the Curriculum
    Lesson 24....................How Do Domestic and International Events Influence the
                            Buying and Selling of Stocks

MCG–Economics and Entrepreneurship
    Lesson 9......................How Much Are Consumers Willing to Pay?

MCG–International Trade
    Lesson 11....................Ripples

Personal Decision Making: Focus on Economics
    Lesson 5......................Price as a Rationing Method: How Does a Market Work?

United States History, Eyes on the Economy, Vol. II
    Unit 7, Lesson 3.........When Greeting Cards Were Too Expensive to Buy and
                            Milk Was Too Costly to Sell

Content Standard 8, Benchmark 2

Capstone
    Unit 2, Lesson 7.........The Market Never Stands Still

Content Standard 8, Benchmark 3

Content Standard 8, Benchmark 4

Content Standard 9, Benchmark 1

Content Standard 9, Benchmark 2

MCG–Economics and Entrepreneurship
    Lesson 5.....................The Role of Entrepreneurs in Our Economy
    Lesson 15...................Competitive Markets

MCG–International Trade
    Lesson 19...................Organization of Petroleum Exporting Students and Teachers

United States History, Eyes on the Economy, Vol. II
    Unit 4, Lesson 1 ....John D. Rockefeller: Nobody Loves a Competitor
    Unit 4, Lesson 2 ....The Economic Effects of 19th Century Monopoly
    Unit 4, Lesson 3 ....Regulation of Business

Content Standard 9, Benchmark 3

Capstone
    Unit 3, Lesson 7 ....When There Isn't Pure Competition

MCG–International Trade
    Lesson 19...................Organization of Petroleum Exporting Students and Teachers

United States History: Focus on Economics
    Lesson 10...................Why Would White Baseball Club Owners Sign Black Players?

Content Standard 9, Benchmark 4

Capstone
    Unit 3, Lesson 7 ....When There Isn't Pure Competition

MCG–Economics and Entrepreneurship
    Lesson 5.....................The Role of Entrepreneurs in Our Economy
    Lesson 15...................Competitive Markets

United States History, Eyes on the Economy, Vol. II
    Unit 3, Lesson 1 ....The Changing U.S. Economy
    Unit 3, Lesson 3 ....Entrepreneurship Case Study: Andrew Carnegie
    Unit 4, Lesson 1 ....John D. Rockefeller: Nobody Loves a Competitor

Content Standard 10, Benchmark 1

Economics and the Environment
    Lesson 6.....................It's Fine as Long as It's Mine—All Mine!
    Lesson 12...................Negotiate or Take Them to Court?
    Lesson 16...................The Extinction of Chickens and Mosquitos—Not!

Economies in Transition: Command to Market
    Lesson 3.....................A Tale of Two Countries
    Lesson 8.....................Public to Private

Content Standard 10, Benchmark 2

Learning from the Market: Integrating the Stock Market Game™ across the Curriculum
    Lesson 2.....................What is a Corporation?
    Lesson 3.....................What is a Stock? or Who Owns McDonalds?
    Lesson 20...................How Businesses Obtain Financing

MCG–Economics and Entrepreneurship
    Lesson 13....................What Type of Business Should I Start?

United States History: Focus on Economics
    Lesson 5......................The Buffalo Are Back

Content Standard 11, Benchmark 1

Civics and Government: Focus on Economics
    Lesson 7......................Who Should Control the Money Supply—The U.S. Congress or
        the Federal Reserve?

Content Standard 11, Benchmark 2

Civics and Government: Focus on Economics
    Lesson 7......................Who Should Control the Money Supply—The U.S. Congress or
        the Federal Reserve?

Focus: High School Economics
    Lesson 20....................Money, Interest, and Monetary Policy

United States History, Eyes on the Economy, Vol. II
    Unit 6, Lesson 3 ....The Federal Reserve System Is Established
    Unit 7, Lesson 1 ....Whatdunit? The Great Depression Mystery

Content Standard 12, Benchmark 1

Learning from the Market: Integrating the Stock Market Game™ across the Curriculum
    Lesson 11....................Getting Rich is Child's Play—The News About Compound Interest

MCG–Economics and Entrepreneurship
    Lesson 14....................Borrowing Decisions and Expected Returns

Personal Finance Economics: Wallet Wisdom
    Lesson 8......................The Credit Connection

Content Standard 12, Benchmark 2

Focus: High School Economics
    Lesson 20....................Money, Interest, and Monetary Policy

MCG–Economics and Entrepreneurship
    Lesson 14....................Borrowing Decisions and Expected Returns

Personal Finance Economics: Wallet Wisdom
    Lesson 6......................Saving Selection
    Lesson 8......................The Credit Connection

Content Standard 12, Benchmark 4

Capstone
    Unit 6, Lesson 3 ....Making a Macro Model: Investment

Economics and the Environment
    Lesson 15....................Halloween Treats and Nonrenewable Resources
    Lesson 16....................The Extinction of Chickens and Mosquitos—Not!

Content Standard 13, Benchmark 2

MCG–Economics and Entrepreneurship
Lesson 16....................The Demand for Labor

Personal Decision Making: Focus on Economics
Lesson 4......................A Student's Potential in the Labor Market: It's a Matter of Supply and Demand Personal Finance Economics 9-12: Wallet Wisdom

United States History, Eyes on the Economy, Vol. II
Unit 3, Lesson 2.........The Economics of Immigration
Unit 9, Lesson 1.........Women in the U.S. Work Force: From Rose the Riveter to the Loan Officer

Content Standard 13, Benchmark 3

Capstone
Unit 3, Lesson 5.........Why Do Some People Make More

Focus: High School Economics
Lesson 11....................Rich Man, Poor Man

MCG–Economics and Entrepreneurship
Lesson 16....................The Demand for Labor

Personal Decision Making: Focus on Economics
Lesson 4......................A Student's Potential in the Labor Market: It's a Matter of Supply and Demand

United States History, Eyes on the Economy, Vol. II
Unit 9, Lesson 1.........Women in the U.S. Work Force: From Rose the Riveter to the Loan Officer

United States History: Focus on Economics
Lesson 11....................Where Did the African-American Middle Class Come From?

Content Standard 13, Benchmark 4

Capstone
Unit 3, Lesson 5.........Why Do Some People Make More

Choices & Changes: Choice Making, Productivity, and Planning
Part 3, Day 2..............Planning to Choose

Civics and Government: Focus on Economics
Lesson 11....................What Can the Government Do About Unemployment?

Focus: High School Economics
Lesson 11....................Rich Man, Poor Man

Personal Decision Making: Focus on Economics
Lesson 4......................A Student's Potential in the Labor Market: It's a Matter of Supply and Demand

Content Standard 13, Benchmark 5

Civics and Government: Focus on Economics

Content Standard 15, Benchmark 3

Content Standard 15, Benchmark 4

Content Standard 15, Benchmark 5

Content Standard 15, Benchmark 6

Capstone
Unit 6, Lesson 3 ....Making a Macro Model: Investment

Economics and Entrepreneurship
Lesson 14....................Borrowing Decisions and Expected Returns

Content Standard 15, Benchmark 7

United States History, Eyes on the Economy, Vol. II
Unit 3, Lesson 1 ....The Changing U.S. Economy

World History: Focus on Economics
Lesson 9.....................The Industrial Revolution

Content Standard 16, Benchmark 1

Capstone
Unit 4, Lesson 11 ....Thinking Economically About the Environment

Civics and Government: Focus on Economics
Lesson 4......................What Are the Economic Functions of Government?

Economics and the Environment
Lesson 6......................It's Fine as Long as It's Mine—All Mine!
Lesson 8......................Don't Rain on My Parade!

Economies in Transition: Command to Market
Lesson 6......................All for One, One for All—Well Maybe: Problems Within a
Tightly Controlled Industrial Structure

Focus: High School Economics
Lesson 13....................Third-Party Costs and Benefits

Geography: Focus on Economics
Lesson 11....................The Lancaster Landfill

United States History, Eyes on the Economy, Vol. II
Unit 4, Lesson 2 ....The Economic Effects of 19th Century Monopoly
Unit 4, Lesson 3 ....Regulation of Business
Unit 7, Lesson 4 ....The New Deal

United States History: Focus on Economics
Lesson 5......................The Buffalo Are Back

Content Standard 16, Benchmark 2

Capstone
Unit 4, Lesson 2 ....The Constitution and You
Unit 4, Lesson 3 ....The Influence of Economic Problems on the Constitution

Civics and Government: Focus on Economics
Lesson 1......................How Has the Constitution Shaped the Economic System in
the United States?
Lesson 4......................What Are the Economic Functions of Government?

Economics and the Environment
    Lesson 6.....................It's Fine as Long as It's Mine—All Mine!
    Lesson 12...................Negotiate or Take Them to Court?
    Lesson 16...................The Extinction of Chickens and Mosquitos—Not!

Geography: Focus on Economics
    Lesson 11...................The Lancaster Landfill

Content Standard 16, Benchmark 3

Capstone
    Unit 4, Lesson 2 ....The Constitution and You

Civics and Government: Focus on Economics
    Lesson 4......................What Are the Economic Functions of Government?

Economics and the Environment
    Lesson 6......................It's Fine as Long as It's Mine—All Mine!
    Lesson 12....................Negotiate or Take Them to Court?
    Lesson 16....................The Extinction of Chickens and Mosquitos—Not!

Geography: Focus on Economics
    Lesson 11....................The Lancaster Landfill

Content Standard 16, Benchmark 4

Capstone
    Unit 4, Lesson 11 ....Thinking Economically About the Environment

Civics and Government: Focus on Economics
    Lesson 4......................What Are the Economic Functions of Government?
    Lesson 9......................How Are Economic Solutions to Pollution Different
        From Political Solutions?
    Lesson 10....................Why Does the Federal Government Give Money to State and
        Local Governments?

Economics and the Environment
    Lesson 8......................Don't Rain on My Parade!

Focus: High School Economics
    Lesson 13....................Third-Party Costs and Benefits

United States History, Eyes on the Economy, Vol. II
    Unit 8, Lesson 1 ....Growth After World War II

Content Standard 16, Benchmark 5

Capstone
    Unit 4, Lesson 11 ....Thinking Economically About the Environment

Civics and Government: Focus on Economics
    Lesson 1......................How Has the Constitution Shaped the Economic System in
        the United States?
    Lesson 4......................What Are the Economic Functions of Government?

Content Standard 16, Benchmark 6

Content Standard 16, Benchmark 7

Content Standard 16, Benchmark 8

Capstone
Unit 4, Lesson 4 ....Why Do We Want Government? Public Versus Private Goods

Civics and Government: Focus on Economics
Lesson 4......................What Are the Economic Functions of Government?
Lesson 10...................Why Does the Federal Government Give Money to State
and Local Governments?

Economics and the Environment
Lesson 7......................We're All in This Together!

Focus: High School Economics
Lesson 12...................Public Goods and Services

Content Standard 16, Benchmark 9

Economics and the Environment
Lesson 7......................We're All in This Together!
Lesson 8......................Don't Rain on My Parade!
Lesson 9......................Weighing the Pluses and the Minuses: Benefit-Cost Analysis

Economies in Transition: Command to Market
Lesson 5......................Economic Transition: The Role of the State

Focus: High School Economics
Lesson 15...................When There Isn't Pure Competition

Personal Decision Making: Focus on Economics
Lesson 8......................The Role of Government: Who Needs It?

United States History, Eyes on the Economy, Vol. II
Unit 7, Lesson 4 ....The New Deal

Content Standard 17, Benchmark 1

Civics and Government: Focus on Economics
Lesson 13...................Whose Interest Is Being Served?

Focus: High School Economics
Lesson 14...................Public Choice: Economics Goes to Washington and into
the Voting Booth

United States History, Eyes on the Economy, Vol. II
Unit 9, Lesson 2 ....Why Does the Federal Government Overspend Its Budget?

Content Standard 17, Benchmark 2

Civics and Government: Focus on Economics
Lesson 13...................Whose Interest Is Being Served?
Lesson 15...................Why Would Government Limit International Trade?

Focus: High School Economics
Lesson 14...................Public Choice: Economics Goes to Washington and into
the Voting Booth

Content Standard 17, Benchmark 3

Content Standard 17, Benchmark 4

Content Standard 17, Benchmark 5

Content Standard 18, Benchmark 1

Economies in Transition: Command to Market
Lesson 4.......................Klips and Kupons

Geography: Focus on Economics
Lesson 4.......................International Interdependence
Lesson 7.......................Places and Production
Lesson 8.......................GDP and Life Expectancy

Learning from the Market: Integrating the Stock Market Game™ across the Curriculum
Lesson 23....................Business Cycles and the Stock Market

MCG: International Trade
Lesson 7.......................Interpreting Trade Data: Graphs and Charts

Content Standard 18, Benchmark 2

Geography: Focus on Economics
Lesson 7.......................Places and Production
Lesson 8.......................GDP and Life Expectancy

Learning from the Market: Integrating the Stock Market Game™ across the Curriculum
Lesson 18....................I've Got the Workin' in the Chalk-Mark Factory, Increasing My Productivity Blues
Lesson 19....................How Do Savings and Investment Affect Economic Growth?

United States History, Eyes on the Economy, Vol. II
Unit 8, Lesson 1 ....Growth After World War II

Content Standard 18, Benchmark 3

Civics and Government: Focus on Economics
Lesson 6.......................How Can Changes in the Federal Government's Budget Stabilize the Economy?

Focus: High School Economics
Lesson 19....................Aggregate Supply and Aggregate Demand: The Sum of Their Parts, and More

United States History, Eyes on the Economy, Vol. II
Unit 7, Lesson 2 ....Where Did All the Income Go?

Content Standard 18, Benchmark 4

Civics and Government: Focus on Economics
Lesson 6.......................How Can Changes in the Federal Government's Budget Stabilize the Economy?

Focus: High School Economics
Lesson 19....................Aggregate Supply and Aggregate Demand: The Sum of Their Parts, and More

Learning from the Market: Integrating the Stock Market Game™ across the Curriculum
Lesson 23....................Business Cycles and the Stock Market

Content Standard 18, Benchmark 5

Content Standard 19, Benchmark 1

Content Standard 19, Benchmark 2

Content Standard 19, Benchmark 4

Content Standard 19, Benchmark 6

Content Standard 19, Benchmark 7

Content Standard 19, Benchmark 8

Economies in Transition: Command to Market
Lesson 4.......................Klips and Kupons

Focus: High School Economics
Lesson 18....................Economic Ups and Downs

United States History, Eyes on the Economy, Vol. II
Unit 6, Lesson 1 ....Raising Inflation on the Farm
Unit 6, Lesson 2 ....Free Silver or a Cross of Gold

Content Standard 19, Benchmark 9

Personal Finance Economics 9-12: Wallet Wisdom
Lesson 10....................Changes and Choices

Content Standard 20, Benchmark 1

Capstone
Unit 5, Lesson 4 ....If It Doesn't Work—Fix It

Civics and Government: Focus on Economics
Lesson 6.......................How Can Changes in the Federal Government's Budget
Stabilize the Government?

United States History, Eyes on the Economy, Vol. II
Unit 7, Lesson 4 ....The New Deal

Content Standard 20, Benchmark 2

Capstone
Unit 5, Lesson 4 ....If It Doesn't Work—Fix It

Civics and Government: Focus on Economics
Lesson 6.......................How Can Changes in the Federal Government's Budget
Stabilize the Government?

Focus: High School Economics
Lesson 19....................Aggregate Supply and Aggregate Demand: The Sum of
Their Parts, and More

United States History, Eyes on the Economy, Vol. II
Unit 7, Lesson 4 ....The New Deal

Content Standard 20, Benchmark 3

Capstone
Unit 5, Lesson 4 ....If It Doesn't Work—Fix It

Content Standard 20, Benchmark 4

Capstone
Unit 5, Lesson 4 ....If It Doesn't Work—Fix It

Civics and Government: Focus on Economics
    Lesson 6......................How Can Changes in the Federal Government's Budget
                                Stabilize the Economy?

United States History, Eyes on the Economy, Vol. II
    Unit 9, Lesson 2.........Why Does the Federal Government Overspend its Budget?

Content Standard 20, Benchmark 5

Civics and Government: Focus on Economics
    Lesson 5......................How Has Federal Government Spending Changed?

United States History, Eyes on the Economy, Vol. II
    Unit 9, Lesson 2.........Why Does the Federal Government Overspend Its Budget?

Content Standard 20, Benchmark 6

United States History, Eyes on the Economy, Vol. II
    Unit 9, Lesson 2.........Why Does the Federal Government Overspend Its Budget?

Content Standard 20, Benchmark 7

Focus: High School Economics
    Lesson 20....................Money, Interest, and Monetary Policy

United States History, Eyes on the Economy, Vol. II
    Unit 6, Lesson 2.........Free Silver or A "Cross of Gold"

Content Standard 20, Benchmark 8

Civics and Government: Focus on Economics
    Lesson 7......................Who Should Control the Money Supply—The U.S. Congress or the
                                Federal Reserve

Focus: High School Economics
    Lesson 20....................Money, Interest, and Monetary Policy

United States History, Eyes on the Economy, Vol. II
    Unit 6, Lesson 3.........The Federal Reserve System Is Established

Content Standard 20, Benchmark 9

Focus: High School Economics
    Lesson 20....................Money, Interest, and Monetary Policy